A Minister, a Priest, and a Rabbi

Al Tapper & Peter Press

MJF BOOKS

NEW YORK

Published by MJF Books
Fine Communications
322 Eighth Avenue
New York, NY 10001

A Minister, a Priest, and a Rabbi
Library of Congress Control Number 2002104921
ISBN 1-56731-546-1

Copyright © 2000 by Al Tapper and Peter Press

This edition published by arrangement with Andrews McMeel
Publishing.

Manufactured in the United States of America on acid-free paper

MJF Books and the MJF colophon are trademarks of Fine Creative
Media, Inc.

BG   10 9 8 7 6 5 4 3 2 1

To my girlfriend, Laura, who would laugh hysterically at any joke and then say, "I don't get it."

Al Tapper

I dedicate this book to my good friend and coauthor, Al Tapper, who conceived of this series of books, who rewrote 95 percent of all the jokes, who designed all the covers, and who is currently holding a gun to my head.

Peter Press

Acknowledgments

We wish to acknowledge "Bill Gates," whose name is in quotes because he, to us, most represents the Internet, wherein lie incredible amounts of information available to us, the authors, for our profitable consumption. Many other sources were also used in this compilation of this book and almost every joke has been rewritten by the authors so that they would be palatable to middle America, thereby making it possible for us to sell the most books and to generate the greatest amount of income. After all, we are a capitalist society. However, since we are also a litigious society, we hereby give credit to anyone who may have created any joke printed in this book, whether they can prove it or not, or to paraphrase the immortal words of Henny Youngman, don't sue us—please!

The pope had a meeting of all his bishops and cardinals at the Vatican one day, and during a break, one cardinal was at a window getting some air when he noticed Jesus walking up the Vatican steps. He thought he must be seeing things, so he got a couple of his colleagues to confirm that yes, Jesus was walking up the Vatican steps. The men then got the pope to see for himself that yes, Jesus was walking up the steps. One cardinal spoke. "Your worship, Lord Jesus Christ is coming here to the Vatican to visit us. What should we do?" To which the pope replied, "Look busy."

$\mathcal{A}$ dying man, not wishing to leave anything to chance, invited a minister, a priest, and a rabbi to his bedside and handed each of them an envelope containing $25,000 in cash. He made them each promise that after his death and during his repose, they would place the envelopes in his coffin so that he could perform charitable deeds in the afterlife. A week later the man died. At the funeral, the minister, priest, and rabbi each concealed an envelope in the coffin and bid the man farewell. By chance these three met several years later. Soon the minister, feeling guilty, blurted out a confession, saying that there was only $10,000 in the envelope he placed in the coffin. Rather than waste all the money, he thought he would send it to a mission in South America. He asked for the other clergymen's forgiveness. The priest, moved by the gentle minister's sincerity, confessed that he too had kept some of the money for a worthy charity. His envelope, he admitted, had only $8,000 in it. He said he too could not bring himself to waste the money so frivolously when it could be used to benefit others. By this time the rabbi was seething with self-righteous outrage. He expressed his deep disappointment in the felonious behavior of his colleagues. "I am the only one who kept his promise to the dying man. I want you both to know that the envelope I placed in the coffin contained my personal check for the entire $25,000."

A priest and a rabbi who had been the best of friends for years were always arguing the finer points of their respective theologies, trying to prove the other one wrong. One day they were riding in a car and they got cut off by a drunk driver. The car flew off the road, rolled five times end over end, and came to rest on its roof. The priest and rabbi crawled from the wreckage and were amazed they were alive. As the priest crossed himself, he noticed the rabbi doing the same. The priest shouted, "Praise be! You've seen the light!" "What?" said the rabbi. "You've crossed yourself! You have seen the true way! This is wonderful!" "Cross myself? No, no, no. I was just checking that everything was okay and in order—spectacles, testicles, wallet, and checkbook."

𝒜 priest and a rabbi were discussing their respective collection boxes and how the money was split. The priest said, "We give four-fifths to Christian charities and the last fifth we keep for ourselves and for the vicarage." The rabbi said, "Each week my wife and two children take one corner of a tablecloth and put all the money into the middle. We toss the money very high into the air up to God. Whatever He wants, He takes, and whatever falls back to earth we keep!"

A priest and a rabbi were taking the same flight and had seats next to each other. After a while, the priest turned to the rabbi and asked, "Is it still a requirement of your faith that you not eat pork?" The rabbi responded, "Yes, that is still a requirement of our faith." The priest then asked, "Have you ever eaten pork?" The rabbi replied, "Yes, on one occasion I did succumb to the temptation and tasted pork." The priest nodded in understanding and went on with his reading. A while later the rabbi spoke up and asked the priest, "Father, is it still a requirement of your church that you remain celibate?" The priest replied, "Yes, that is still very much a part of our faith." The rabbi then asked him, "Father, have you ever fallen to the temptations of the flesh?" The priest replied, "Yes, Rabbi, on one occasion I was weak and broke my vow of celibacy." The rabbi nodded understandingly for a moment and then said, "A lot better than pork, isn't it?"

The pastor of the local church walked into the neighborhood pub to use the restroom. The place was hopping with music and dancing, and the lights were turned down low. When the customers saw the pastor the room quieted down and the lights were turned up as he walked over to the bartender and asked, "May I please use the restroom?" The bartender replied, "I really don't think you should." "Why not?" the pastor asked, "I really need to use the restroom!" "Well, I don't think you should. There is a statue of a naked woman in there—and she's only covered by a fig leaf!" "Nonsense," said the pastor. "I'll look the other way!" So the bartender showed the clergyman the door at the top of the stairs and he proceeded to the restroom. After a few minutes he came back out and the lights were again turned low and the whole place was hopping with music and dancing. He went to the bartender and said, "Sir, I don't understand. When I came in here the lights were low and the place was hopping with music and dancing. I assume, out of respect for my position, the room brightened, the music stopped, and the room became absolutely quiet. I went to the restroom and now the place is hopping again." "Well, now you're one of us!" said the bartender. "But I still don't understand," said the puzzled pastor. "You see," said the bartender, "every time the fig leaf is lifted on the statue, the music starts and the lights dim in the whole place."

Three seminarians about to undergo their final test before ordination were taken by an old priest into a luxurious room and told to strip and then tie a small bell around their organ. Suddenly a ravishing girl entered the room, and one bell *ding-a-linged* furiously. "To the showers, Fogarty!" barked the old priest. Then, as the girl tantalizingly undressed, the father heard *ding-a-ling, ding-a-ling.* "Sorry about that, O'Brien. The showers for you, too." Finally alone with the naked lovely, the remaining seminarian watched as the girl writhed seductively around him; yet he somehow remained calm, and the bell, silent. "Praise the Lord and congratulations, Featherstone!" the priest exulted. "You made it! Now, go join those weaker souls in the showers."

Ding-a-ling.

Three men were standing in line to get into heaven one day. Apparently it had been a pretty busy day, so St. Peter had to tell the first one, "Heaven's getting pretty close to full today, and I've been asked to admit only people who have had particularly horrible deaths. So, what's your story?" The first man replied, "Well, for a while I've suspected my wife has been cheating on me, so today I came home early to try to catch her red-handed. As I came into my twenty-fifth floor apartment, I could tell something was wrong, but all my searching around didn't reveal where this other guy could have been hiding. Finally, I went out to the balcony and, sure enough, there was this man hanging off the railing, twenty-five floors above ground! I was really mad, so I started beating on him and kicking him, but wouldn't you know it, he wouldn't fall off. So finally I went back into my apartment and got a hammer and started hammering on his fingers. Of course, he couldn't stand that for long, so he let go and fell— but even after twenty-five stories, he fell into the bushes, stunned, but okay. I couldn't stand it anymore so I ran into the kitchen, grabbed the fridge, and threw it over the edge, where it landed on him, killing him instantly. But all the stress and anger got to me and I had a heart attack and died there on the balcony." "That sounds like a pretty bad day to me," said St. Peter, and he let the man in. The second man came up and St. Peter explained to him about heaven being full. Again he asked for his story. "It's been a very strange day. You see, I live on the twenty-sixth floor of my apartment building, and every morning I do my exercises out on my balcony. Well, this morning I must have slipped or something, because I fell over the edge. But I got lucky and caught the railing of the balcony on the floor below me. I knew I couldn't hold on for very long.

Suddenly this man burst out onto the balcony. I thought for sure I was saved, but all of a sudden he started beating on me and kicking me. I held on the best I could until he ran into the apartment and grabbed a hammer and started pounding on my hands. Finally, I just let go, but again, I got lucky and fell into the bushes below, stunned but all right. Just when I was thinking I was going to be okay, this refrigerator came falling out of the sky and crushed me instantly, and now I'm here." Once again, St. Peter had to concede that that sounded like a pretty horrible death. The third man came to the front of the line. Again St. Peter explained that heaven was full and asked for his story. "Picture this," said the third man, "I'm hiding naked inside a refrigerator . . ."

Tommy O'Connor went to confession and said, "Forgive me, Father, for I have sinned." "What have you done, Tommy O'Connor?" "I had sex with a girl." "Who was it, Tommy?" "I cannot tell you, Father, please forgive me for my sin." "Was it Mary Margaret Sullivan?" "No, Father, please forgive me for my sin, but I cannot tell you who it was." "Was it Catherine Mary McKenzie?" "No, Father, please forgive me for my sin." "Well then, it must have been her sister, Sarah Martha McKenzie?" "No, Father, please, Father, please forgive me, I cannot tell you who it was." "Okay, Tommy, go say five Hail Marys and four Our Fathers and you will be absolved of your sin." Tommy walked out to the pews, where his friend Joey was waiting. "What did ya get?" asked Joey. "Well, I got five Hail Marys, four Our Fathers, and three good leads."

$\mathcal{A}$ minister, a priest, and a rabbi went into the Sahara Desert. The minister took a bottle of wine, the priest took an umbrella, and the rabbi took a car door. $\mathcal{A}$ stranger noticing this asked why they were taking the things they were carrying. The minister said, "In case I get thirsty." The priest said, "In case it rains." And the rabbi said, "Because if it gets hot I can roll down the window."

A minister, a priest, and a rabbi climbed up to the top of a cliff. At the top they met a Hindu Wise Man. The man said, "If you can take your watch and drop it down the cliff, catch it again, bring it back up completely intact, and you're uninjured, God will grant you eternal life." The minister thought he could do it, so he dropped his watch and ran all the way down to the bottom of the cliff and came back up with his watch in pieces. The priest thought he could do it as well, so he dropped his watch and jumped down the cliff and came back with his watch intact, but he was on a stretcher. The rabbi thought he could do it as well, so he dropped his watch and walked slowly down the cliff and he came back up with his watch working perfectly. The Hindu said, "How in the world did you do that?" "I set my watch back two hours," said the rabbi.

During a papal audience, a businessman approached the pope and made this offer: If he changed the last line of the Lord's Prayer from "Give us this day our daily bread" to "Give us this day our daily chicken," then KFC would donate $10 million to Catholic charities. The pope declined. Two weeks later the man approached the pope again, this time with a $50 million offer. Again, the pope declined. A month later the man offered $100 million. This time the pope accepted. At a meeting of the cardinals, the pope announced his decision in the good news/bad news format: "The good news is that we have one hundred million dollars. The bad news is that we lost the Wonder Bread account!"

$\mathcal{A}$ man talking to God asked him, "God, why did you make women so beautiful?" God replied, "So that you would find them attractive." Then the man asked, "God, but why did you have to make them so dumb?" God replied, "So that they would find you attractive!"

Dear Congregant:

During the Christmas season, many individuals expressed concern over the seating arrangements in the church. In order for us to place you in a seat which will best suit you, we ask you to complete the following questionnaire and return it to the Rectory as soon as possible.

1. I would prefer to sit in the:
   __ Talking section
   __ No talking section

2. If talking, which subcategory do you prefer?
   __ Stock market __ Sports __ Medicine
   __ Fashion news __ Sex
   __ Other (please specify)

3. Which of the following would you like to be near so that you might receive free professional advice:

__ Lawyer __ Doctor

__ Accountant __ Stockbroker

4. I want a seat located:

__ Near my in-laws

__ Far from my in-laws

__ Far from my ex-in-laws

5. I wish to be seated in a seat where:

__ I can sleep during services

__ I can sleep during the priest's sermon (additional charge)

A nun goes to see her doctor complaining of constant hiccups. Within a few minutes she comes running out, screaming and crying, and bumps into a guy walking into the doctor's office. The guy walks in and says, "Doc, what's with the nun?" The doctor says, "Oh, I just told her she's pregnant." The guy says, "The nun's pregnant?" "No," says the doctor, "but I cured her hiccups."

"Pilot to tower . . . pilot to tower . . . I am 300 miles from land . . . 600 feet over water . . . and running out of fuel . . . please instruct!" "Tower to pilot . . . tower to pilot . . . repeat after me: 'Our Father which art in heaven . . .'"

A mother and her daughter were at the gynecologist's office. The mother asked the doctor to examine her daughter. "She has been having some strange symptoms and I'm worried about her," the mother said. The doctor examined the daughter carefully and then announced, "Madam, I believe your daughter is pregnant." The mother gasped, "That's nonsense! Why, my little girl has nothing whatsoever to do with men." She turned to the girl. "You don't, do you, dear?" "No, Mumsy," said the girl. "Why, you know that I have never so much as kissed a man!" The doctor looked from mother to daughter and back again. Then, silently, he stood up and walked to the window, staring out.

He continued staring until the mother felt compelled to ask, "Doctor, is there something wrong out there?" "No, Madam," said the doctor. "It's just that the last time anything like this happened, a star appeared in the East."

The preacher said that, for a change, he would call out a word and anyone who could think of a hymn that involved that word should just start singing and the congregation would all join in. He called out *wood* and in just a second ten people started singing "The Old Rugged Cross." He called out *love* and a little six-year-old started singing "Jesus Loves Me." He then called out *sex*. Not a sound. Again he called out *sex*. A little old lady in the back row suddenly stood up and started singing "Memories."

An Irish priest was at the altar one dreary Sunday morning addressing his congregation, vehemently declaring that alcohol was the work of the devil. "As an example," he stated during his sermon, "if you were to lead a donkey to a bowl of water and a bowl of whiskey, from which would he drink?" A grizzled old man at the back of the church spoke up. "Aye, Father, he'd drink from the water." The priest, elated, said, "Very good! And can you tell me *why* he'd drink from the water?" The same Irishman at the back of the church replied, "Sure I can tell ya why, Father. Because he's an ass!"

Every Sunday morning everyone in tiny Smithville wakes up early and goes to the one local church. Before the service starts, the townspeople, as is their custom, sit in their pews and talk about their lives, their families, and so on. Suddenly, one morning, Satan appeared at the altar! Everyone started screaming and running for the front entrance, trampling each other in their determined efforts to get away from evil incarnate. Soon everyone had left the church except for one man, who sat calmly in his pew, seemingly oblivious to the fact that God's ultimate enemy was in his presence. This confused Satan a bit. Satan walked up to the man and said, "Hey, don't you know who I am?" The man said, "Sure I do." Satan said, "Well, aren't you afraid of me?" The man said, "Nope. Sure ain't." Satan, perturbed, said, "And why aren't you afraid of me?" The man said, "Well, I've been married to your sister for twenty-five years."

$\mathcal{B}$ill, Frank, and John were waiting to be cleared for entrance into heaven. St. Peter walked up to Bill and asked, "How many times did you cheat on your wife? And remember, I will know the truth." Bill thought for a moment and replied, "Well, sir, I'd say around forty times." "Fine," said St. Peter, "you may enter heaven, but you will have to drive that green Ford Pinto over there for the rest of eternity." St. Peter approached Frank and asked the same question. Frank answered, "Sir, I believe it was around twenty times." "Good," said St. Peter, "you may also now enter heaven, and you will be driving that red Buick." St. Peter walked up to John and repeated the question. Without pause, John answered, "Never!" St. Peter peered at him and asked, "Never? Are you sure?" "I have never been unfaithful to my wife, sir," he replied. "Excellent," replied St. Peter, "you may now enter heaven, and you will be driving that beautiful gold Rolls-Royce." Grinning from ear to ear, John approached the car, but when he reached the car, he suddenly dropped his head on the roof and began to cry. St. Peter rushed over and asked, "What's the matter, John? You have never cheated on your wife, you've gained entrance into heaven, and you will be driving a Rolls-Royce for the rest of eternity! Why are you crying?" John looked up at St. Peter and replied while sobbing uncontrollably, "I just saw my wife drive by on a skateboard!"

Two nuns, Sister Mary and Sister Helena, are traveling through Europe in their car. They get to Transylvania and are stopped at a traffic light. Suddenly, a diminutive vampire jumps onto the hood of the car and hisses through the windshield. "Quick, quick," shouts Sister Mary, "what shall I do?" "Turn the windshield wipers on, that will get rid of the abomination," says Sister Helena. Sister Mary switches them on, knocking the vampire around, but he clings on and hisses again at the nuns. "What shall I do now?" she shouts. "Switch on the windshield washer. I filled it with holy water at the Vatican," says Sister Helena. The vampire screams as the water burns his skin, but he clings on and hisses again. "Now what?" shouts Sister Mary. "Show him your cross!" shouts Sister Helena. Sister Mary opens the window and screams: *"Get off my fucking car!!"*

$\mathcal{A}$n archaeologist was digging in the Negev Desert in Israel and came upon a casket containing a mummy. After examining it he called the curator of a prestigious natural history museum. "I've just discovered a three-thousand-year-old mummy of a man who died of heart failure!" the excited scientist exclaimed. The curator replied, "Bring him in. We'll check it out." A week later the amazed curator called the archaeologist. "You were right about the mummy's age and cause of death. How in the world did you know?" "Easy. There was a piece of paper in his hand that said 'Ten thousand shekels on Goliath.'"

Things you never hear in church:

1. Hey! It's my turn to sit in the front pew.

2. I was so enthralled, I never noticed your sermon went twenty-five minutes over time.

3. Personally, I find witnessing much more enjoyable than golf.

4. I've decided to give our church the $500 a month I used to send to TV evangelists.

5. I volunteer to be the permanent teacher for the junior high Sunday school class.

6. Forget the denominational minimum salary. Let's pay our pastor more money so he can live like we do.

7. I love it when we sing hymns I've never heard before!

8. Since we're all here, let's start the service early.

9. Pastor, we'd like to send you to this Bible seminar in the Bahamas.

10. Nothing inspires me and strengthens my commitment like our annual fund-raising campaign!

*A*Baptist preacher had really roused his predominantly black congregation one Sunday only to end his sermon with this admonition: "It has come to my attention that someone in this congregation has maligned the piano player by calling him a motherfucker and I would like to know *right now* who in this assembly would do a thing like that, calling the piano player a motherfucker."

You could hear a pin drop except for a few nervous coughs, when, at the back of the church, a small man jumped to his feet and, pointing in the direction of the choir, said, "Preacher, I'd like to know who called that motherfucker a piano player!"

Two ministers greeted each other every Sunday morning as they rode their bicycles to their respective churches. Then one Sunday one of the ministers was walking. "My, what happened to your bike?" asked the other. "Can you believe that someone in my congregation stole it?" "No!" said his fellow minister, then an idea struck him. "You want to know how to get your bike back? Give a fire-and-brimstone sermon on the Ten Commandments, and when you get to the part about 'Thou shall not steal,' just look out into the congregation and see who looks guilty." The following Sunday the two ministers met and they both had their bikes. "Hey, I see my suggestion worked after all," said one. "Well, sort of. I was going along real good on the Ten Commandments and when I got to the part about adultery I remembered where I left my bike!"

A Muslim was killed in a car accident. He arrived at the gates of heaven. St. Peter said, "I'm St. Peter. Welcome to heaven." The Muslim said, "Nice to meet you, St. Peter, but I'm a Muslim and I want to meet Mohammed." St. Peter said, "Sure, no problem. Climb up that ladder behind you and you will meet Mohammed." The Muslim climbed up the ladder, got to the top, and there was Moses. Moses said, "Hi, I'm Moses. Welcome to heaven." The Muslim was very excited. "Moses, it's such an honor to meet you. But like I told St. Peter, I'm a Muslim, and I really want to meet Mohammed." Moses said, "No problem. Climb up the ladder behind you and you will meet Mohammed." The Muslim climbed up the ladder, but when he got to the top he couldn't see anything but bright light. He saw this figure before him and asked, "Who are you?" The figure responded, "I am God. Nice to meet you. Welcome to heaven." God walked over and shook his hand. The Muslim was stunned; he could hardly speak. He said to God, "Sir, it is such an honor to meet You. I can't believe it. This place is great. But I'm a Muslim and, no disrespect intended, but I really want to meet Mohammed." God said, "Ohh . . . you're here to see Mohammed. I see. No problem. Have a seat. Get comfortable. Can I get you some coffee or something to eat?" The Muslim said, "I would love a cup of coffee." God yelled into the kitchen, "Hey, Mohammed, two coffees!"

During Yom Kippur, a rabbi is so overwhelmed with religious fervor that he drops to his knees, puts his forehead to the ground, and says, "Lord, before you I am nothing." Not to be outdone, the cantor too gets on his knees and puts his forehead to the ground and says, "Before you, Lord, I am nothing." Moved by their humility, a man in the fourth row steps into the aisle. He falls down on his knees, puts his forehead to the ground, and says, "Before you, Lord, I am nothing." The rabbi, noting the gesture, elbows the cantor. "So," he whispers, "look who thinks he's nothing."

A guy named Joe finds himself in dire trouble. His business has gone bust and he's in serious financial straits. He's so desperate that he decides to ask God for help. He begins to pray. "God, please help me. I've lost my business and if I don't get some money, I'm going to lose my house as well. Please let me win the Lotto." Lotto night comes and somebody else wins it. Joe again prays. "God, please, let me win the Lotto! I've lost my business and my house, and I'm going to lose my car as well." Lotto night comes and Joe still doesn't win. Once again, he prays. "My God, why have you forsaken me? I've lost my business, my house, and my car. My wife and children are starving. I don't often ask you for help and I have always been a good servant to you. *Please* just let me win the Lotto one time so I can get my life back in order." Suddenly there is a blinding flash of light as the heavens open and Joe is confronted by the voice of God Himself. "Joe, meet me halfway on this. Buy a ticket!"

One summer a Jewish man moved into a Catholic neighborhood. Every Friday the Jew would drive the Catholics crazy because, while they were eating fish, he would be outside grilling steaks. The Catholics asked him to stop; in fact, they tried to convert him. Finally, by threats and pleading, the Catholics succeeded. They took the Jew to a priest, who sprinkled holy water on the Jew and intoned: "Born a Jew, raised a Jew, now a Catholic." The Catholics were ecstatic—no more steak aroma filling the air every Friday evening. But the next Friday evening, the scent of barbecue once again filled the air. The Catholics rushed over to the convert's house in order to remind him of his new Catholic "diet." When they arrived, they saw him standing over the grill. He was sprinkling water on the meat and they heard him say, "Born a cow, raised a cow, now a fish!"

An elderly priest invited a young priest over for dinner. During the meal the young priest couldn't help noticing how attractive and shapely the housekeeper was. Over the course of the evening he started to wonder if there was more between the elderly priest and the house-keeper than met the eye. Reading the young priest's thoughts, the elderly priest volunteered, "I know what you must be thinking, but I assure you, my relation-ship with the housekeeper is purely professional." About a week later the housekeeper came to the elderly priest and said, "Father, ever since the young priest came to dinner, I've been unable to find the beautiful silver gravy ladle. You don't suppose he took it, do you?" The priest said, "Well, I doubt it, but I'll write him a letter just to be sure." So he sat down and wrote, "Dear Father, I'm not saying that you did take a gravy ladle from my house, and I'm not saying you did not take a gravy ladle. But the fact remains that one has been missing ever since you were here for dinner." Several days later, the elderly priest received from the young priest a letter that read, "Dear Father, I'm not saying that you do sleep with your housekeeper, and I'm not saying that you do not sleep with your housekeeper, but the fact remains that if you were sleeping in your own bed, you would have found the gravy ladle."

One Easter morning, a Sunday school teacher asked her class if they knew the origins of this special day. One young man responded immediately, "It's opening day for the Yankees and Mets!" Not wishing to stifle creative thinking, the teacher responded, "Yes, that is correct! But I had something else in mind." A young girl then stood and remarked, "This is the day we get nice new clothes and go find the eggs from the Easter Bunny." "That's right," said the teacher, "but there's something else just a little more important." A young man then jumped up and yelled, "I know, I know! After Jesus died on the cross, some of his friends buried him in a tomb they called a sepulcher." The teacher thought, "I don't believe it, someone actually knows." The little boy continued, "And three days later Jesus arose and opened the door of his tomb and stepped out." "Yes, yes," said the teacher, "go on, go on!" And the youngster said, "And if He sees His shadow, we have six more weeks of *winter*."

$\mathcal{A}$ young man of seven had been staring at a plaque located on a prominent wall of the church for some time, so the pastor walked up and stood beside him. Gazing up at the plaque, he said quietly, "Good morning, Johnny." "Good morning, Pastor," replied the young man, not taking his eyes off the plaque. "Sir, what is this?" Johnny asked. "Well, son, these are all the people who have died in the service," replied the pastor. Soberly, they stood together staring up at the large plaque. Little Johnny's voice broke the silence when he asked quietly, "Which one, sir, the eight thirty or the ten thirty?"

In Mississippi there was a popular minister of a large congregation who, after giving a particularly moving sermon, said, "Friends, I have been hearing some very nasty rumors!" Total silence fell across the congregation. "One of you, my faithful followers, has been saying that I am a member of the Ku Klux Klan. This is not true! I am now asking that the guilty party stand up and confess and apologize before the congregation." A pretty woman sitting in the first pew stood up. "Preacher, I'm really sorry, I don't know how this came to be. All I said was that you were a wizard under the sheets."

$\mathcal{A}$ priest was called away for an emergency. Not wanting to leave the confessional unattended, he called his rabbi friend from across the street and asked him to cover for him. The rabbi told him he wouldn't know what to say, but the priest told him to come on over and he'd stay with him for a little bit and show him what to do. The rabbi arrived, and he and the priest sat in the confessional together. In a few minutes a woman came in and said, "Father, forgive me, for I have sinned. I have committed adultery." The priest said, "How many times?" The woman said, "Three times." The priest said, "Say two Hail Marys, put $5.00 in the poor box, and sin no more." A few minutes later a man entered the confessional. He said, "Father, forgive me, for I have sinned." The priest said, "What did you do?" The man said,

"I have committed adultery." The priest asked, "How many times?" The man replied, "Three times." The priest said, "Say two Hail Marys, put $5.00 in the poor box, and sin no more." The rabbi told the priest that he thought he had it, so the priest left. A few minutes later another woman entered and said, "Father, forgive me, for I have sinned." The rabbi said, "What did you do?" The woman replied, "I have committed adultery." The rabbi asked, "How many times?" The woman replied, "Once." The rabbi said, "Go do it two more times. We have a special this week, three for $5.00."

Father O'Grady was saying his good-byes to his parishioners after Sunday morning services as he always did when Mary Clancy came up to him in tears. "What's bothering you, dear?" inquired Father O'Grady. "Oh, Father, I've got terrible news," replied Mary. "What is it, my child?" asked the priest. "Well, my husband passed away last night, Father." "Oh, Mary," said the priest, "that's terrible. Tell me, did he have any last requests?" "Well, yes, he did, Father," replied Mary. "What did he ask?" She replied, "He said, 'Please, Mary, put down the gun . . .'"

A missionary in the deepest part of the Amazon suddenly finds himself surrounded by a menacing group of natives. Upon surveying the situation, he says quietly to himself, "Oh, God, I'm screwed!" Then a ray of light appears from heaven and a voice booms out, "No, you are *not* screwed. Pick up that stone at your feet and bash in the head of the chief standing in front of you." So the missionary picks up the stone and proceeds to bash the living hell out of the chief. As he stands above the lifeless body, breathing heavily and surrounded by one hundred and fifty natives all with a look of shock on their faces, God's voice booms out again, "Okay, *now* you're screwed!"

Three guys found themselves in hell: Bob, Dave, and Phil. A little confused at their situation, they were startled to see a door in the wall open, and behind the door was perhaps the ugliest woman they had ever seen. She was three feet, four inches tall, dirty, and you could smell her over the brimstone. The voice of the devil was heard, "Bob, you have sinned! You are condemned to spend the rest of eternity in bed with this woman!" And Bob was whisked through the door to his torment by a group of lesser demons. This, understandably, shook up the other two and so they both jumped when a second door opened and they saw an even more horrifying woman. She was over seven feet tall, monstrous, covered in thick black hair, and flies circled her eyes. The voice of the devil was heard. "Dave, you have sinned! You are condemned to spend the rest of eternity in bed with this woman!" And Dave, like Bob, was whisked off. Phil, now alone and fearing the worst, stood like a stone as the third door inched open. He strained to see the figure of . . . Cindy Crawford! Delighted, Phil jumped up, taking in the sight of this beautiful woman, barely dressed in a skimpy bikini. Then he heard the voice of the devil saying, "Cindy, you have sinned . . ."

Three married couples went to a pastor to inquire if they could join his church. The preacher was pleased with their interest, but he insisted that they pass a test. "To show your sincerity," he told them, "you must practice total abstinence for two weeks." Two weeks later the three couples returned to the church. "Well, how did you do?" the pastor asked the first couple. "We've been married for twenty years," the man answered. "It was no problem." "Great. I'd like to welcome you to our church," the pastor said. He then turned to the second couple and asked how they had managed. "It wasn't easy," the woman said. "We've been married for only three years, so we had some difficult moments, but we didn't give in." "Wonderful," the pastor replied. "I'd like to welcome you to our church." He then turned to the last couple, who were newlyweds. "I can't lie," the man said. "We were both doing fine until this morning at breakfast when she dropped her napkin on the floor. We both reached down to pick it up and our eyes met. Our hearts were so overcome with passion that we gave in right then and there." "I understand, my children," the pastor said, "but I'm afraid I can't let you come to our church." "That's okay," the man replied. "We can't go back to that restaurant, either."

A woman finds herself outside the pearly gates, where she is greeted by St. Peter. "Am I where I think I am?" she exclaims. "It's so beautiful! Did I really make it to heaven?" St. Peter replies, "Yes, my dear, these are the gates to heaven. But you must do one thing before you can enter." Very excited, the woman asks what she must do to pass through the gates. "Spell a word," St. Peter replies. "What word?" she asks. "Any word," answers St. Peter. "It's your choice." The woman promptly replies, "The word I will spell is *love*. L-o-v-e." St. Peter congratulates her on her good fortune of making it into heaven and asks her if she will take his place at the gates for a moment while he goes to pray. "I'd be honored," she says, "but what should I do if someone comes while you are gone?" St. Peter instructs her to require any newcomers to spell a word, just as she had done. So the woman takes St. Peter's chair and observes the angels soaring around her, when lo and behold, a man approaches the gates. It is her husband! "What happened?" she cries. "Why are you here?" Her husband explains, "I had a few drinks after I left your funeral and I got into an automobile accident. Now I am here, ready to join you in heaven." "Not just yet," the woman replies. "First you must spell a word." "What word?" he asks. "Czechoslovakia."

There were three couples returning by plane from vacation when their plane crashed. Then, lo and behold, each couple found themselves in an elevator tended by an angel going up to the pearly gates to face St. Peter. St. Peter asked the first man, "Sir, is it true you loved money so much that you married a woman named Penny?" And when the man answered yes, he and his wife were told to go down to hell. The next couple came before St. Peter. St. Peter said, "Is it true, sir, that you loved alcohol so much that you married a woman named Sherry?" And when the second man answered yes, St. Peter told him to go on down to hell. After witnessing this, the third man grabbed his wife Fanny's hand and said to the angel, "Down, please."

A minister, a priest, and a rabbi are all in a boat together fishing. The minister says to the others, "I think I am going to go over to the shore and sit down." So he gets out of the boat, walks across the water, and sits down on the shore. Then the priest says to the rabbi, "I think I am going to go over there and join him." So he does the same as the minister and sits next to him on the shore. The rabbi thinks to himself, "Well, if they can do it, so can I!" So he climbs out of the boat but he sinks immediately. The minister says to the priest, "Do you think we should have told him where the rocks were?"

Two nuns are ordered to paint a room in the convent. The last instruction of the mother superior is that they must not get a drop of paint on their habits. After conferring about this for a while, the two nuns decided to lock the door of the room, strip off their habits, and paint in the nude. In the middle of the project there comes a knock at the door. "Who is it?" calls one of the nuns. "Blind man," replies a voice from the other side of the door. The two nuns look at each other and shrug, and, deciding that no harm can come from letting a blind man into the room, they open the door. "Nice breasts," says the man. "Where do you want the blinds?"

priest and a rabbi get into a car accident and it's a bad one. Both cars are totally demolished, but, amazingly, neither of the clerics is hurt. After they crawl out of their cars, the rabbi sees the priest's collar and says, "So you're a priest. I'm a rabbi. Just look at our cars. There's nothing left, but we are unhurt. This must be a sign from God. God must have meant that we should meet and be friends and live together in peace and harmony the rest of our days." The priest replies, "I agree with you completely. This must be a sign from God." The rabbi continues, "And look at this. Here's another miracle. My car is completely demolished, but this bottle of kosher wine didn't break. Surely God wants us to drink this wine and celebrate our good fortune." Then he hands the bottle to the priest. The priest agrees, takes seven or eight big swigs, and hands the bottle back to the rabbi. The rabbi takes the bottle, immediately puts the cap on, and hands it back to the priest. The priest asks, "Aren't you having any?" The rabbi replies, "No, I think I'll wait for the police."

A minister, a priest, and a rabbi were discussing the unforeseen possibility of their sudden death. One of the clergymen said, "We will all die someday, and none of us really knows when, but if we did know we would all do a better job of preparing ourselves for that inevitable event." The other two shook their heads in agreement with this comment. Then the rabbi said to the group, "What would you do if you knew you only had four weeks of life remaining before your death and Judgment Day?" The minister said, "I would go out into my community and preach the Gospel to those that have not yet accepted the Lord into their lives." The rabbi then asked the priest what he would do and the priest replied, "I would dedicate all of my remaining time to serving God, my family, my church, and my fellow man with a greater conviction." "That's wonderful!" the other two commented. Finally, the minister and priest asked the rabbi what he would do and he said, "I would go to my mother-in-law's house for the four weeks." The minister and priest were puzzled by this answer and asked, "Why your mother-in-law's home?" The rabbi smiled and said, "Because that would be the longest four weeks of my life!"

There was a pope who was greatly loved by all of his followers. He was a man who led with gentleness, faith, and wisdom. His passing was grieved by the entire world. As the pope approached the gates of heaven, St. Peter greeted him in a firm embrace. "Welcome, Your Holiness. Your dedication and unselfishness in serving your fellow man during your life has earned you great stature in heaven. You may pass through the gates without delay and are granted free access to all parts of heaven. You are also granted an open-door policy and may, at your own discretion, meet with any heavenly leader, including the Father, without prior appointment. Is there anything that Your Holiness desires?"

"Well, yes," the pope replied, "I have often pondered some of the mysteries that have puzzled and confounded theologians through the ages. I would love to see what was actually said without the dimming of memories over time." St. Peter immediately ushered the pope to the heavenly library and explained how to retrieve the various documents. The pope was thrilled and settled down to review the history of man's relationship with God. Two years later a scream of anguish came from the beloved pope. Immediately, several of the saints and angels came running to the pope's side to learn the cause of his dismay. There they found the pope pointing to a single word on the parchment, repeating over and over, "There's an *R!* There's an *R,* look! There's an *R.* The word is *celebrate,* not *celibate!*"

$\mathcal{A}$ cardinal and two bishops are on a transcontinental flight. They each have a copy of the morning newspaper and are each doing the crossword puzzle. One of the bishops asks, "Do either of you know a four-letter word ending in $\mathcal{K}$ that means intercourse?" The other bishop says, "That's easy. It's *talk*." The cardinal says, "Can I borrow an eraser?"

A preacher was telling his congregation that anything they could think of, old or new, was discussed somewhere in the Bible, and that the entirety of the human experience could be found there. After the service, he was approached by a woman who said, "Preacher, I don't believe the Bible mentions PMS." The preacher replied that he was sure it must be there somewhere and that he would look for it. The following week after the service, the preacher called the woman aside and showed her a passage that read, "And Mary rode Joseph's ass all the way to Bethlehem."

One day little Johnny asked his mother for a new bike. His mother said, "At Christmas you send a letter to Santa to ask for what you want, don't you?" "Yes," replied Johnny, "but it isn't Christmas." His mother said, "Yes, but you can send a letter to Jesus and ask him." Johnny sat down with a pen and paper and started his letter: "Dear Jesus, I've been a good boy and I would like a new bike. Your friend, Johnny." He read it over and didn't like it, so he decided to start a new letter: "Dear Jesus, Sometimes I'm a good boy and I would like a new bike." Again, he didn't like it and decided to write another letter: "Dear Jesus,

I thought about being a good boy and I would like a new bike." He thought awhile and decided that he didn't like that one, either. He left and went walking around, depressed, when he went by a house with a small statue of Mary in the front yard. He picked up the statue and hurried home. He put the statue under the bed and started his new letter: "Dear Jesus, If you want to see your mother again, send me a new bike! Your friend, Johnny."

One bright summer's day a young priest was playing a round of golf with one of the nuns from his church. At the first hole the priest took a mighty swing at the ball and missed. "Damn!" he said. "Father! You should not use such language!" said the nun. "Of course. I am sorry, Sister. I was frustrated, but it won't happen again." His second shot off the third tee went out of bounds and the priest said, "Damn! Missed again!" "Father!" "Oh, sorry, Sister . . . it won't happen again." A few holes later, the priest said, "Damn! Missed again!" "Father, if you persist in using such foul language, God will surely strike you down!" said the nun. "Yes, of course. Sorry, Sister." Still later, the priest cried, "God dammit! Missed again!" Just then the sky darkened as huge, dark clouds appeared overhead. Suddenly, the clouds parted and a single bolt of lightning streaked to earth, killing the nun instantly. A low, troubled voice rumbled from the clouds, "Damn . . . missed again."

A group of people are touring the White House in Washington, D.C. As the tour ends they are waiting in line to sign the visitors' register. A group of nuns are in line to sign the book, followed by a Jewish family with their young son, Sheldon. As they near the visitors' register, young Sheldon loses patience and runs ahead to sign the book. However, his mother stops him and admonishes him by saying, "Wait till the nun signs, Shelly!"

The pope comes out of a meeting in New York. He gets into his limo and the limo driver pulls out and gets on the freeway. The pope taps on the glass and says, "Would you mind if I drove?" The limo driver says, "I'm really not supposed to do that." The pope replies, "I have my license and I won't tell a soul." The limo driver still won't do it. Finally the pope says, "What if I told you that if you let me drive, you'll be guaranteed to go straight to heaven when you die?" The limo driver pulls over and they switch places. The pope takes off. Fifty mph, sixty mph. He's flying down the road at ninety mph when a cop pulls out and chases him down. The cop gets out, taps on the window, and the pope rolls it down. The cop looks at him and says, "Hold on one minute." He goes back and radios dispatch, saying, "What are we supposed to do if we pull over someone *really* important?" The dispatcher says, "Like who?" The cop says, "I mean somebody *really, really* important!" The dispatcher says, "Who is it?" The cop says, "I mean this guy is *really, really, really* important!" The dispatcher yells, "*Who is it?*" The cop says, "I don't know, but the pope is his chauffeur!"

$\mathcal{A}$ guy is at the pearly gates waiting to be admitted while St. Peter leafs through a big book to see if the guy is worthy of entering. St. Peter goes through the book several times, furrows his brow, and says to the guy, "You know, I can't see that you did anything really good in your life, but you never did anything really bad, either. Tell you what. Maybe I'm missing something. If you can tell me of one *really* good deed that you did in your life, you're in." The guy thinks for a moment and says, "Well, I was driving down the highway and I saw a group of KKK bikers sexually assaulting a poor girl. I slowed down my car to see what was going on, and sure enough there they were, about fifty of them torturing this woman. Infuriated, I got out of my car, grabbed a tire iron from my trunk, and walked straight up to the leader of the gang, a huge guy with a studded leather jacket and a chain running from his nose to his ear. As I walked up to the leader, the bikers formed a circle around me. So I ripped the leader's chain off his face and smashed him over the head with the tire iron. Then I turned around and yelled to the rest of them, 'Leave this poor, innocent girl alone. You're all a bunch of sick, deranged animals! Go home before I teach you all a lesson in pain!'" St. Peter, impressed, says, "Really? When did this happen?" "Oh, about two minutes ago."

One day, after a near eternity in the Garden of Eden, Adam calls out to God, "Lord, I have a problem." "What's your problem, Adam?" God asks. "Lord, I know you created me and have provided for me and surrounded me with this beautiful garden and all of these wonderful animals, but I'm just not happy." "Why is that, Adam?" comes the reply from the heavens. "Lord, I am lonely." "Well, Adam, in that case, I have the perfect solution. I shall create a woman for you." "What's a woman, Lord?" "This woman will be the most intelligent, sensitive, caring, and beautiful creature I have ever created. She will be so intelligent that she can figure out what you want before you ask for it. She will be so sensitive that she will know your every mood and how to make you happy. Her beauty will rival that of the heavens and earth. She will be the perfect companion for you," replies the heavenly voice. "But this is going to cost you, Adam." "How much?" Adam asks. "It'll cost you an arm and a leg." Adam ponders this for some time with a look of deep concern on his face. Finally, Adam says to God, "Ehhh, what can I get for a rib?"

One rainy night a priest was driving and couldn't see anything out of the windshield. He stopped at a hotel and asked for a room. About an hour later there was a knock on his door. "Quick, quick!" screamed the hotel manager. "There's a terrible flood. Get yourself into the rescue boat before you drown!" But the priest remained calm. "The Lord is my Savior, and He will save me." Not long afterward, the water rose to the second floor. A second boat sailed past the priest's window and the captain looked inside. "Good God, Father, jump in here before you die!" "The Lord is my Savior, He will save me," replied the priest. Sure enough, the flood raged higher and higher, until the priest was forced out onto the hotel roof. A nearby helicopter saw the man's plight and dangled a rope ladder down to him. "Hurry up!"

yelled the pilot. "Grab onto the rope!" The priest smiled. "The Lord is my Savior, He will . . ." All of a sudden a gigantic lightning bolt struck the priest in the head. Next thing he knew, the priest was at the gates of heaven, seated before God himself. "My Lord!" he wailed. "Why did you forsake me?" "Forsake you! I sent you two boats and a helicopter!"

A minister, tired of tending to the needs and demands of his flock Sunday after Sunday after Sunday, decided to play hooky. One Sunday he loaded his squirrel rifle and headed out for a hunt. He intended to walk through the woods totally alone, and just shoot any squirrel that might present itself. Toward late afternoon, the preacher was walking back home along an old logging road. He had long since exhausted his ammunition and had not hit one squirrel. Still, he was feeling relaxed and refreshed. On turning a corner, however, he came face to face with one very large bear. This bear was huge and he was appetizingly eyeing the preacher. The preacher dropped to his knees and bowed his head. "Oh, Lord!" he said. "Have mercy on me, a sinner. I have done wrong. But if I could ask just one thing of you, Lord, please make this bear a Christian!" At this point the preacher heard a strange thump. He lifted his eyes to see the mighty bear on his knees in the dirt. His massive paws came together in a prayerful manner and he bowed his head. Then the bear spoke: "Oh, Lord, bless this meal I am about to receive . . ."

St. Peter takes a day off from his duties at the gates to heaven and asks Jesus if he would stand in for him. While booking in the new arrivals, Jesus notices an old man in line who seems familiar. When this man gets to the front, Jesus asks him his name. "Joseph" is the reply, which makes Jesus more inquisitive. "Occupation?" is the next question. The reply is "Carpenter." Jesus is now getting quite excited and asks, "Did you have a little boy?" The answer is "Yes." "Did he have holes in his wrists and ankles?" asks Jesus. "Yes," comes the reply. Jesus looks at the old man in front of him and with tears in his eyes shouts, "Father, Father!" The old man looks puzzled and after a moment replies, "Pinocchio?"

Two men died and went to heaven. God greeted them and said, "I'm sorry, gentlemen, but your mansions aren't ready yet. Until they are, I can send you back to earth as whatever you want to be." "Great!" said the first guy. "I want to be an eagle soaring above a magnificent landscape!" "No problem," replied God. *Poof!* The guy was gone. "And what do you want to be?" God asked the other guy. "I'd like to be one cool stud!" was the reply. "Easy," replied God, and the other guy was gone. After a few minutes, their mansions were finished, and God sent an angel to fetch them back. "You'll find them easily," he said. "One of them is soaring above the Grand Canyon, and the other one is on a snow tire somewhere in Detroit!"

$\mathcal{A}$ minister, a priest, and a rabbi die in a car crash. They go to heaven for orientation. They are all asked, "When you are in your casket, and friends, family, and congregants are mourning over you, what would you like to hear them say?" The minister says, "I would like to hear them say that I was a wonderful husband, a fine spiritual leader, and a great family man." The priest says, "I would like to hear that I was a wonderful teacher and a servant of God who made a huge difference in people's lives." The rabbi replies, "I would like to hear them say, 'Look, he's moving!'"

Three monks are meditating in the Himalayas. One year passes in silence and one of them says to the others, "Pretty cold here." Another year passes and the second monk says, "You know, you are quite right." Another year comes to pass, and the third monk says, "Hey, I'm gonna leave unless you guys stop talking!"

A man has been walking in the hot desert for about two weeks. Finally, just as he's about to collapse from heat exhaustion, he sees the home of a missionary. Tired and weak, he crawls up to the house and falls on the doorstep. The missionary finds him and nurses him back to health. Feeling better, the man thanks the missionary and continues his trek through the desert. On his way out the door he sees a horse. He goes back to the house and asks the missionary, "Could I borrow your horse and give it back when I reach the nearest town?" The missionary says, "Sure, but there is a special thing about this horse. You have to say, 'Thank God' to make it go, and 'Amen' to make it stop."

Feeling elated and not paying much attention the man says, "Sure. Okay." So he gets on the horse, says, "Thank God," and the horse starts walking. Then he says, "Thank God, thank God," and the horse starts trotting. Feeling secure, the man says, "Thank God, thank God, thank God, thank God," and the horse starts to gallop. Pretty soon he sees this cliff coming up, and he's doing everything he can to make the horse stop. "Whoa, stop, hold on!" Finally he remembers and shouts, "Amen!" The horse stops four inches from the cliff. Then the man leans back in the saddle, wipes his brow, and says, "Thank God."

$\mathcal{F}$ather Joseph went up to Father Michael one afternoon and said, "I am sick of all this clean living. Tonight let's you and me go out and party. We'll carouse, drink, whatever we want." Michael was shocked. "Are you crazy? This is a small town and everyone knows us. Besides, even if they didn't, they would see our clothes and know we are priests." Joseph was ready for this. "Don't be silly. We won't stay in town. We'll go into the city, where nobody knows us, and we'll dress just like everyone else." In the end he managed to persuade Michael and they went out and partied through the night. When they got home at five A.M., Michael's face became pale. "I just thought of something," he said. "We have to confess this." Again, Joseph was ready. "Relax. I told you, I thought this all out in advance. Tomorrow you go into church and into the confessional. I will come in in my regular clothes and confess, and you will absolve me. Then I will put on my garments, you'll come in and confess, and I'll absolve you." Michael was amazed at Joseph's brilliance. And so Joseph went in later that morning and said, "Father, forgive me, for I have sinned. My friend and I went out last night and caroused. We became drunk, had sexual relations with women, used foul language, and danced to wicked music." Michael answered, "God is patient and forgiving, and thus shall I be. Do five Our Fathers and five Hail Marys, and you will be absolved of your sin." A while later their places were reversed as Michael came in and confessed everything in detail. There was a short pause and Joseph answered, "I don't believe this. How *dare* you call yourself a priest? You will do five hundred Our Fathers and five hundred Hail Marys, donate all your money for the next month to the church, and walk around the church five hundred times on your knees asking God's forgiveness. Then come back and we'll discuss absolution, but I make no guarantees." "*What?*" Father Michael was shocked. "What about our agreement?" Joseph replied, "Hey, what I do on my time off is one thing, but I take my job seriously."

Three elderly Catholic women are having coffee one morning. The first woman says, "My grandson is a priest. When he walks in a room everyone calls him 'Father.'" The second woman says, "My grandson is a bishop. When he walks in a room everyone calls him 'Your Grace.'" The third woman, not wanting to be outdone, says, "My grandson is a Cardinal. When he walks into a room everyone says, 'Hey, aren't you Mark McGwire?'"

A couple preparing for a religious conversion meets with the Orthodox rabbi for their final session. The rabbi asks if they have any final questions. The man asks, "Is it true that in the Orthodox tradition men and women don't dance together?" "Yes," says the rabbi. "For modesty reasons, men and women dance separately." "So I can't dance with my own wife?" "No." "Well, okay," says the man, "but what about sex?" "Fine," says the rabbi. "It is a *mitzvah,* or good deed, within the marriage." "What about different positions?" the man asks. "No problem," says the rabbi. "Woman on top?" the man asks. "Why not?" replies the rabbi. "Well, what about standing up?" "No!" says the rabbi. "Why not?" asks the man. "Could lead to dancing," replies the rabbi.

There were four rabbis who had a series of theological arguments, and three were always in accord against the fourth. One day the odd rabbi out, after losing yet another argument by a vote of three to one, decided to appeal to a higher authority. "Oh, God!" he cried. "I know in my heart that I am right and they are wrong! Please give me a sign to prove it to them!" It was a beautiful sunny day, and as soon as the rabbi finished his prayer, a storm cloud moved across the sky above the four rabbis. It rumbled once and dissolved. "A sign from God! See, I am right, I knew it!" cried the rabbi, but the other three disagreed, pointing out that storm clouds form on hot days. So the rabbi prayed again, "Oh, God, I need a bigger sign to show that I am right and they are wrong. So, please God, a bigger sign!" This time four storm clouds appeared and rushed toward each other to form one big cloud. A bolt of lightning slammed into a tree on a nearby hill. "I told you I was right!" cried the rabbi, but the other three insisted that nothing had happened that could not be explained by natural causes. The rabbi was getting ready to ask for a very big sign, but just as he said, "Oh, God," the sky turned pitch-black, the earth shook, and a deep, booming voice intoned, "*He is right!*" The rabbi, righteously indignant, put his hands on his hips, turned to the other three, and said, "Well?" "So," shrugged one of the other rabbis, "now it's three to two."

A man went to church with his wife every Sunday but always fell asleep during the sermon. The wife decided to do something about this, and one Sunday she took a long hatpin to poke him with every time he dozed off. As the preacher got to a part in the sermon where he shouted out, "And who created the world in six days and rested on the seventh," she poked her husband, who came flying out of the pew and screamed, "*Good Lord Almighty!*" The minister said, "That's right, that's right," and went on with his sermon. The man sat back down, muttering under his breath, and later began to doze off again. When the minister got to

"And who died on the cross to save us from our sins," the wife poked him again and he jumped up and shouted, "*Jesus Christ!*" The minister said, "That's right, that's right," and went on with his sermon. The man sat back down and began to watch his wife. When the minister got to "And what did Eve say to Adam after the birth of their second child," the wife, who thought her husband had dozed off again, started to poke him. But he jumped up and said, "If you stick that damn thing in me again I'll break it off!"

Do you know how to make holy water? You take some regular water and you boil the hell out of it!

The pope calls a meeting of all the cardinals. When they have all assembled at the Vatican, he takes them into the meeting hall and states, "I have some really fantastic news and some very terrible news." Of course all the cardinals want to hear the good news first, so the pope tells them, "I have just heard from Jesus Christ. He has returned to the world. The time of judgment is at hand, and our faith in His existence is justified." After the commotion dies down a bit, one of the cardinals speaks up, asking what the terrible news is. The pope replies, "He was calling from Salt Lake City."

$\mathcal{A}$ new priest at his first mass was so nervous he could hardly speak. After mass he asked the monsignor how he had done. The monsignor shook his head and replied, "When I get nervous on the pulpit, I replace the water glass with a glass of vodka. If I start to get nervous, I take a sip." So the next Sunday the priest took the monsignor's advice. At the beginning of the sermon, he got so nervous he downed the whole glass. He proceeded to talk up a storm. Upon returning to his office following mass, he found the following note from the monsignor on the door: "Sip the vodka, *don't* gulp it. There are ten commandments, not twelve. There are twelve disciples, not ten. Jesus was consecrated, not constipated. Jacob wagered his donkey, he did not bet his ass. We do not refer to Jesus Christ and his disciples as J.C. and the Sunshine Boys. David slew Goliath, he did not kick the shit out of him. We do not refer to the cross as the Big T. The recommended grace before a meal is not 'Rub-a-dub-dub, thanks for the grub, yeah, God!' Next Sunday there will be a taffy-pulling contest at St. Peter's, not a peter-pulling contest at St. Taffy's."

A kid is flunking in public school so his parents send him to a Catholic parochial school. All of a sudden in this environment his grades skyrocket to all As. One night at the dinner table his parents ask, "Why were you doing so bad in a public school, and when we switched you to a Catholic school, you did good?" The kid responds, "Because I knew they were serious about school. The first day I walked in they had a guy nailed to a plus sign."

$\mathcal{A}$ man goes to heaven. An angel escorts him around. As they pass different areas, the angel points out the Protestants, the Jews, the Seventh-Day Adventists, the Mormons, and many other groups. They reach a wall one hundred feet high. The man views the wall in awe. The angel responds to the inquiring look, saying, "The Catholics are on the other side. They think they're the only ones up here!"

An old geezer lived near the Ohio River and in a severe flood he was washed away. His friends and family feared that he'd drowned. Miraculously, though, a good Samaritan pulled him out and his life was saved. The old geezer lived many more years, but, unfortunately, he kept telling everyone how he survived the Ohio River floods until they were bored to tears. Finally he died and went up to heaven. St. Peter met him at the pearly gates and said, "Welcome to heaven! We'd like you to be eternally happy, so if there's anything you'd like to do, anything at all, just tell me and we'll fix it up for you." "Thanks," said the old geezer. "I'd sure like to tell a bunch of folks about how I survived the Ohio River floods." St. Peter said, "I'll make the arrangements and get back to you." A few days later, St. Peter contacted the old man and took him to the lecture hall, where he was to give his talk. They both waited backstage while the audience got settled, and the man was pleased to see that it was rather a large crowd. Then St. Peter grabbed the old man's arm. "Now, I don't want to make you nervous, but I've just spotted Noah in the audience."

At the Hebrew school, Goldblatt, the teacher, finished the day's lesson. It was now time for the usual question period. "Mr. Goldblatt," announced little Joey, "there's something I can't figure out." "What's that, Joey?" asked Goldblatt. "Well, according to the Bible, the children of Israel crossed the Red Sea, right?" "Right." "And the children of Israel beat up the Philistines, right?" "Er, right." "And the children of Israel built the Temple in Jerusalem, right?" "Again, you're right." "And the children of Israel left the land of Egypt, and the children of Israel fought unsuccessfully against the Romans, and the children of Israel were always doing something important, right?" "All that is right," agreed Goldblatt. "So what's your question?" "What I want to know is this," demanded Joey. "What were the grown-ups doing all that time?"

mother was teaching her three-year-old daughter the Lord's Prayer. For several evenings at bedtime she repeated it after her mother. One night she said she was ready to go solo. The mother listened with pride as her daughter carefully enunciated each word right up to the end. "And lead us not into temptation," she prayed, "but deliver us some E-mail. Amen."

$\mathcal{A}$ young boy had just gotten his driver's permit and inquired of his father if they could discuss the use of the car. His father took him into his study and said to the boy, "I'll make a deal with you, son. You bring your grades up from Cs to Bs, study your Bible, get your hair cut, and we'll talk about the car." Well, the boy thought for a moment and agreed. After about six weeks the boy came back and again asked his father about the car. Again, they went to his study, where his father said, "Son, I'm real proud of you. You've brought your grades up, you've been studying the Bible, and have even been participating a lot more in the Bible study class on Sunday mornings. But I'm real disappointed that you haven't got your hair cut." The young man paused a moment and then said, "You know, Dad, I've been thinking about that, and in studying the Bible I've noticed that Samson had long hair, Moses had long hair, John the Baptist had long hair, and even Jesus Himself had long hair." To which his father replied, "You're right, son. Did you also notice that they all *walked* everywhere they went?"

Two Irishmen were digging a ditch directly across the street from a brothel. Suddenly, they saw a rabbi walk up to the door, glance around, and duck inside. "Ah, will you look at that?" one ditch digger said. "What's our world coming to when men of the cloth are visitin' such places?" A short time later, a Protestant minister walked up to the door and quietly slipped inside. "Do you believe that?" the workman exclaimed. "Why, 'tis no wonder the young people today are so confused, what with the example clergymen are setting for them." After an hour went by, the men watched as a Catholic priest quickly entered the house. "Oh, what a pity," one of the diggers said, leaning on his shovel. "One of the poor lasses must be ill."

An old man of eighty goes into the confessional and tells the priest, "Forgive me, Father, for I have sinned." The Father asks the nature of his infraction. The old man confesses he made love to two twenty-year-old girls. The priest asks, "How long since your last confession?" The old man replies, "Oh, I've never been to confession. I'm Jewish." The priest queries, "Then why are you telling me this?" The old man replies, "Hell, I'm telling everybody!"

A student was asked to list the Ten Commandments in any order. His answer? "3, 6, 1, 8, 4, 5, 9, 2, 10, and 7."

A Scottish atheist was spending a quiet day fishing when suddenly his boat was attacked by the Loch Ness monster. In one easy flip, the beast tossed him high into the air. Then it opened its mouth to swallow him. As the man sailed head over heels, he cried out, "Oh, my God! Help me!" All at once the scene froze in place and, as the atheist hung in midair, a booming voice came down from the clouds. "I thought you didn't believe in me?" "Come on, God, a minute ago I didn't believe in the Loch Ness monster, either!"

A minister, a priest, and a rabbi are traveling in the Old West. Suddenly they are ambushed and captured by blood-thirsty Indians. All three are tied to stakes. Then out comes the Big Chief. He walks up to the minister and says, "We're going to torture you, burn you, skin you alive, and then use your skin to make a canoe. I will grant you one last request." Without a second thought, the minister asks for a knife. As soon as he gets the knife, he slashes his own throat and dies. "Very brave man," says the Chief. He then walks over to the priest and says, "We're going to torture you, burn you, skin you alive, and then use your skin to make a canoe. I will grant you one last request."

Without a second thought, the priest asks for a knife. As soon as he gets the knife, he slashes his own throat and dies. "Very brave man," says the Chief. He then walks up to the rabbi and says, "We're going to torture you, burn you, skin you alive, and then use your skin to make a canoe. I will grant you one last request." The rabbi thinks about it for a little bit and finally says, "Bring me a fork!" The entire tribe bursts out laughing. The Chief, laughing himself, commands that a fork be given to the rabbi. The rabbi grabs the fork, starts poking himself all over the chest and stomach, and screams, "I hope your canoe sinks!"

$\mathcal{A}$ minister, a priest, and a rabbi were all stuck on a God-forsaken island for a number of years. One day they found a magic lamp! $\mathcal{A}$ genie comes out and says that since there are three of them, they each get one wish. The minister says, "After all these years on this miserable island, I want to go back to San Francisco," and *poof!* He disappears. The priest says, "I agree with the minister, but send me to the Vatican," and *poof!* He too disappears. The rabbi says, "Well, I really don't have any place to go. No family, no friends, and I sort of like this island and I just wish my two buddies were back." *Poof!*

There is a big controversy these days concerning when life begins. In Jewish tradition the fetus is not considered a viable human being until after graduation from medical school.

The chief rabbi of Israel was visiting in Rome and decided to stop in and see his good friend the pope. While there he noticed that the pope had a gold telephone. "What's that?" the rabbi inquired. "It's my direct line to God," the pope replied. "Can I use it?" asked the rabbi. "Of course," said the pope, "but it costs a lot of money—it costs three thousand dollars." The rabbi thought for a moment and then decided that it was worth the expense to be able to talk directly to God. He made his phone call, conducted his business with God, and paid the pope before he left. Some years later the pope found himself in Jerusalem and went to visit the chief rabbi. When he entered the rabbi's office he noticed a gold phone. "Is that what I think it is?" he asked. "Yes, it's *my* direct line to God. After seeing yours, I had one installed." "Can I use it?" asked the pope. "Of course," said the rabbi. So the pope made his call and spoke with God for about an hour, after which he asked the rabbi, "How much do I owe you?" "A dollar eighty-seven," replied the rabbi. "A dollar eighty-seven? How come so cheap?" asked the pope. "Well, it's only a local call."

Olson was the janitor in the First Lutheran Church in Minneapolis. The new minister decreed that all employees should be able to read and write English. The reasoning was that all employees should be able to handle phone calls and write down information for the minister in his absence. Poor Olson! He had left Norway in his youth and had never learned to read and write. Despite his tearful pleas to the minister, he was forced to leave his job as janitor because of his lack of education. In his bitter disappointment, Olson hitchhiked to Seattle and got a job in a fish cannery, where he would not have to worry about reading and writing. He later worked on a fishing boat and, in time, had enough money to buy his own boat. As time went on, Olson's natural thrift and good business sense earned him more boats. He had the opportunity to buy a very big fleet and, recognizing it as a good business opportunity, he found himself going to the bank for a loan. After viewing all of Olson's vast assets, the banker agreed to give him a loan and drew up the papers. He handed them to him to sign and Olson replied, "I'm sorry, but I don't know how to read and write." The astonished banker looked at him in disbelief and declared, "Mr. Olson, I'm astounded. Just think where you would be today if you could read and write!" "Vell," said Olson, "I'd probably be a yanitor in the Lutheran Church in Minneapolis."

A poor little country church down in Kentucky needed a fresh coat of paint desperately. The dedicated congregation raised just enough money through book sales, suppers, car washes, and the like to buy the paint needed to complete the job. The day came when everyone came out to help paint the church. Unfortunately, the pastor had underestimated the amount of paint needed to finish. So he told the painters to start thinning down the paint with water. They did so and began to paint. Yet they saw that they still would not finish the job properly, so they thinned the paint some more. The color of the wall began to turn from a dark green to a lighter shade of green. Just then a big, black thundercloud came out of nowhere and settled directly over the little church. A torrential downpour fell on the little church and completely washed off all the paint. Then a booming voice came down from the cloud: "Repaint! Repaint! And thin no more."

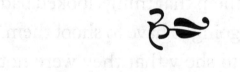

$\mathcal{A}$ minister, a priest, and a rabbi were taken hostage by a team of terrorists. Hours later, the FBI was still standing tough; they wouldn't give the terrorists a million dollars as they requested, nor a getaway car, nor a jumbo jet. The terrorists gathered the three hostages in a corner and informed them that things looked bad and they were going to have to shoot them. Nevertheless, to show that they were not really a bad bunch, they granted each hostage one wish. "Please," says the minister, "for the last two months I've been working on my Easter sermon. What a waste to die now without having delivered it before an audience. I'll go happily if you let me recite my sermon. It's an hour, ninety minutes long, tops." They promise to grant him the wish. "Please," says the priest, "after fifty years I've finally learned the entire Gospel According to Luke. What a waste to die and not recite it to an audience. It's only about fifty-five minutes long—then I'll go happily." The terrorists promise to grant the priest his wish too, and they turn to the rabbi. "Please," says the rabbi, "shoot me first!"

O'Brien loved to play golf and would go out alone to a course and join up with any group that needed a fourth. One day he went to his favorite course and the pro said, "I'm sorry, O'Brien, but the only group I can put you with is one with three rabbis." O'Brien said, "That's fine with me." He joins the group and tees off. His shot is about 200 yards out and off to the right rough. Rabbi Schwartz tees off 300 yards, straight out into the middle of the fairway. Rabbi Gold's shot is about 290, and Rabbi Glickstein's is 320 with a slight draw. O'Brien has trouble with getting out of the rough and four-putts, while the rabbis' approach shots are right on the pin—they two-putt for par. The rest of the round is the same, with the rabbis' scores either par or under par, while O'Brien has a 95. He says to them, "You guys must play and practice all the time." Rabbi Schwartz says, "No, we study all the time and only play once a week. But, on our Sabbath, while we are in Temple, we say a prayer asking

God to give us one good round of golf each week." O'Brien is so impressed that he goes home and tells his wife that they are converting. They study, convert, join a synagogue, and go to services every Saturday. About a year later, O'Brien runs into the threesome at the same course and they invite him to play with them. The game is exactly like last year's. O'Brien is doing nothing right, and the three rabbis are perfect. At the end, O'Brien says to the rabbis, "I don't understand it. I converted, joined a synagogue, and pray every week." Rabbi Gold says, "You joined a synagogue? Which one?" O'Brien says, "Beth El." Rabbi Glickstein says, "No, no, no! Beth El is for *tennis!*"

Short summary of every Jewish holiday: "They tried to kill us, we won, let's eat."

A Jewish grandmother is walking on the beach with her only grandson when a giant wave crashes onshore, sweeping the boy out to sea. The woman looks up to the heavens and says, "Oh, Lord, this is my only grandson, how can you take him away from me like this? My son will not understand. My daughter-in-law will die from grief." Another wave comes by and deposits the boy back at the old woman's feet. The grandmother looks up, points her finger to the heavens, and says, "He had a hat!"

Three elderly Jewish men who were childhood friends meet at a party many years later and start talking. The first one says, "So, did you hear, I've been in the jewelry business. I've been very, very successful. In fact, I even changed my name to Mr. Diamond." The second man says, "I've also been very successful and I've been in the precious metals business. I changed my name to Mr. Silver." The two look at the third man and say, "So?" The third man says, "Well, I was a tailor. At first I didn't do too well. First I was a tailor for men, then I tried being a tailor for women, but I had no luck. So one Friday night when I was at the synagogue, I prayed to

God, 'Please, God, find a good business for me and I'll make you a partner.'" So the other two looked at him and said, "So?" He responded, "What's the matter, you never heard of Lord and Taylor?"

A man wonders if having sex on the Sabbath is a sin because he is not sure if sex is work or play. He asks a priest for his opinion on this question. The priest says, after consulting the Bible, "My son, after an exhaustive search I am positive sex is work and is not permitted on Sundays." The man thinks, "What does a priest know of sex?" He goes to a minister—a married man, experienced—for the answer. He queries the minister and receives the same reply. Sex is work and not for the Sabbath. Not pleased with the reply, he seeks out the ultimate authority—a man of thousands of years of tradition and knowledge—a rabbi. The rabbi ponders the question and states, "My son, sex is definitely play." The man replies, "Rabbi, how can you be so sure when so many others tell me sex is work?" The rabbi softly says, "If sex were work, my wife would have the maid do it."

Late one night, a burglar broke into a house he thought was empty. He tiptoed through the living room but suddenly froze in his tracks when he heard a loud voice say, "Jesus is watching you!" Silence returned to the house, so the burglar crept forward again. "Jesus is watching you!" the voice boomed again. The burglar stopped dead again. He was frightened. Frantically he looked all around. In a dark corner he spotted a birdcage and in the cage was a parrot. He asked the parrot, "Was that you who said Jesus is watching me?" "Yes," said the parrot. The burglar breathed a sigh of relief and asked the parrot, "What's your name?" "Clarence," said the bird. "That's a dumb name for a parrot," sneered the burglar. "What idiot named you Clarence?" The parrot said, "The same idiot who named the Rottweiler Jesus."

Between moments of dispensing wisdom, it seems that historical religious leaders had also learned software programming. One day a great contest was held to test their skills. After days and days of fierce competition, only two leaders remained for the last day's event: Jesus and Mohammed. The judge described the software application required for the final test and gave the signal to start writing code. The two contestants feverishly typed away on their keyboards. Routines, classes, and applications flew by on their screens at incredible speeds. Windows, dialogs, and other intricate graphics began forming on their monitors. The clock showed that the contest would soon be finished. Suddenly, a bolt of lightning flashed and the power went out. After a moment it came back on—just in time for the clock to announce that the last competition was over. The judge asked the two contestants to reveal their finished software. Mohammed angrily said that he'd lost it all in the power outage. The judge turned to the other competitor. Jesus smiled, clicked a mouse, and a dazzling application appeared on his screen. After just a few moments, the judge was clearly impressed and declared Jesus the victor. When asked why the decision was made, the judge pointed out the unique characteristic that set the winner apart from all the other leaders: Jesus saves.

A minister, a priest, and a rabbi are walking down the street on a hot day and are quite thirsty. They pass a busy bar and want to go in and get a drink, but they have no money. But the minister comes up with an idea that he thinks might work. So he goes in alone, telling the others that if his idea works, they can all get free drinks. He orders his drink, and when he's finished with it, the bartender gives him his tab. The minister says, "But, son, I already paid for the drink!" The bartender says, "I'm terribly sorry, Reverend, but it's really busy in here and I must have forgotten." The minister goes out and tells the priest and the rabbi what happened, so the priest goes in next. The priest orders his drink and then informs the bartender that he had already paid when the bartender asks him for the money. Again, the bartender apologizes. Finally the rabbi goes in and orders his drink. Again, the bartender gives him the tab and the rabbi tells him, "Son, I paid you when I ordered the drink." "I'm terribly sorry, Rabbi," says the bartender, "I don't know what's wrong with me, but you're the third man of the cloth that I've done that to." "I'm sorry, son," says the rabbi, "but I'm in a terrible hurry. Just give me my change for the twenty dollars and I'll be on my way!"

Over the massive front doors of a church, these words were inscribed: THE GATE OF HEAVEN. Below that was a small cardboard sign which read: PLEASE USE OTHER ENTRANCE.

A man was brought to Mercy Hospital and went in for coronary surgery. The operation went well and the groggy man regained consciousness. A Sister of Mercy was waiting by his bed. "Mr. Smith, you're going to be just fine," the nun said while patting his hand. "We do have to know, however, how you intend to pay for your stay here. Are you covered by insurance?" "No, I'm not," the man whispered hoarsely. "Can you pay in cash?" "I'm afraid I can't, Sister." "Do you have any close relatives, then?" "Just my sister in New Mexico," he replied, "but she's a spinster nun." "Nuns are not spinsters, Mr. Smith," the nun replied. "They are married to God." "Okay," the man said with a smile. "Then you can bill my brother-in-law."

$\mathcal{A}$ team of archaeologists were excavating in Israel when they came upon a cave. Written on the wall of the cave were the following symbols: a dog, a donkey, a shovel, a fish, and a Star of David.

They decided that this was a unique find and the writings were at least more than three thousand years old. They chopped out the piece of stone and had it brought to the museum, where archaeologists from all over the world came to study the ancient symbols. They held a huge meeting after months of conferences to discuss the meaning of the markings. The president of their society stood up and pointed at the first drawing and said, "This looks like a dog. We can judge that this was a highly intelligent race as they knew how to have animals for companionship. To prove this statement you can see that the next symbol resembles a donkey. So they were even smart enough to have animals help them till the soil. The next drawing looks like a shovel of some sort, which means they even had tools to help them. Even further proof of their high intelligence is the fish, which means that if they had a famine and their crops failed, they would take to the sea for food. The last symbol appears to be the Star of David, which means they were evidently Hebrews." The audience applauded enthusiastically and the president smiled and said, "I'm glad to see that you are all in agreement with the interpretation." Suddenly a little old Jewish man stood up in the back of the room and said, "I object to every word. The real explanation of what the writings say is quite simple. First of all, everyone knows that Hebrews don't read from left to right, but from right to left . . . Now, look again. It now says: 'Holy mackerel, dig the ass on that bitch!'"

A woman went to the post office to buy stamps for her Christmas cards. "What denomination?" asked the clerk. "Oh, good heavens! Have we come to this?" asked the woman. "Well, give me fifty Baptist and fifty Catholic."

On a very cold, snowy Sunday in February only the minister and one farmer arrived at the village church. The minister said, "Well, I guess we won't have a service today." The farmer replied, "Heck, if only one cow shows up at feeding time, I feed it."

After having been commissioned by God to take a survey of how man was doing on earth, St. Peter now stood before his boss ready to present his findings. "Tell me, Peter, what have you found out?" God asked. "I'm very sorry to have to tell you this, but the people are behaving in a sinful manner. There's drugs, alcohol, murders, you name it—a regular Sodom and Gomorrah. But the worst is this new obsession with premarital sex. According to my survey, 88 percent of the population is doing it. I'm afraid it has reached epidemic proportions." "Hmmm," God said thoughtfully, "do you have any recommendations as to what should be done to put an end to this unacceptable sexual behavior?" "I think we should send a message to everyone on earth who engages in premarital sex. The contents of that message should tell them exactly what will happen to them on Judgment Day if they do not stop this type of activity." "That is an effective solution," God stated, "but I think that instead of punishing those who practice premarital sex, we should reward those who refrain from it. Let's send a letter that's personally signed by me to each of these good people." Do *you* know what the letter said? No? I guess *you* didn't get one either, huh?

During a children's sermon, Rabbi Bloomberg asked the children what "Amen" means. A little boy raised his hand and said, "It means tha-tha-tha-that's all, folks!"

*A*fter the church service a little boy told the minister, "When I grow up I'm going to give you some money." "Well, thank you," the minister replied, "but why?" "Because my daddy says you're one of the poorest preachers we've ever had."

minister's wife invited some people from their congregation to dinner. At the table the minister turned to his six-year-old daughter and said, "Would you like to say the blessing?" "I wouldn't know what to say," she replied. "Just say what you hear Mommy say," the minister said. The little girl bowed her head and said, "Dear Lord, why on earth did I invite all these boring people to dinner?"

Past the pearly gates in heaven there are two lines for deceased husbands. One line is marked HENPECKED HUSBANDS, the other, WORE-THE-PANTS HUSBANDS. On this particular day there is a huge line in front of the HENPECKED HUSBANDS sign, but only a lone soul in the WORE-THE-PANTS HUSBANDS line. One of the henpecked asks the odd man out how he came to be in that line. "My wife told me to stand here," he replies.

*A*n Irish man was getting ready to jump to his death from a bridge when a priest walked past. The man turned to the priest and said, "Don't try to stop me, Father, I'm going to jump." "Don't jump," said the priest. "It can't be that bad. Think of the life you have yet to live." "That's one of the reasons I'm jumping!" said the man. "Well, if that won't stop you, think about your family!" said the priest. "That's another reason!" said the man. "Well, think about your job!" said the priest. "There's another reason!" said the man. "Well, if that won't stop you, think about St. Patrick!" said the priest. "Who's that?" asked the man. "Jump, you Protestant bastard!"

Officer Patrick Murphy of the New York City Police Department answers a call on his radio and reports to the scene of a car accident in the Queens-Midtown Tunnel. Officer Murphy notes that a new Buick had its front end merged with the rear end of a Chrysler. The driver of the Buick was Father Francis O'Boyle; the driver of the Chrysler was Rabbi Isaac Goldstein. After Officer Murphy verifies that Rabbi Goldstein has suffered no physical injuries in the accident he walks back to survey the damage to each vehicle. Then Officer Murphy walks over to Father O'Boyle and asks him, "Tell me, Father, just how fast was the rabbi going when he backed into you?"

Jesus is preaching to a mob that is about to stone a whore. He says to the group: "*Let he who is without sin cast the first stone.*" At that moment a woman picks up a large rock and throws it at the whore. Jesus turns to the old woman and says, "I'm trying to make a point here, Mom."

$\mathcal{A}$ man dies and finds himself at the pearly gates being greeted by St. Peter. St. Peter informs the man that he can have one wish granted as he enters heaven. The man says his wish is to ask the Virgin Mary one question. St. Peter looks a little stunned but says that it is an easy wish to fulfill. He takes the man to Mary and explains what the man wants. Mary says that she is honored to grant the man his wish and asks what his question is. The man says that in all the images he has seen of her, the paintings, sculptures, frescoes, and carvings, she always looks so sad. His question is why does she look so sad? Mary looks around to see if anyone else is listening and then leans over and whispers in the man's ear. "Well, to tell you the truth, I really wanted a girl."

Two elderly spinster women were sitting together in the front pew of a church listening to a fiery preacher. When the preacher condemned the sin of lust, these two ladies cried out at the top of their lungs, "Amen, Brother!" When the preacher condemned the sin of stealing, they yelled again, "Preach it, Reverend!" And when the preacher condemned the sin of lying, they jumped to their feet and screamed, "Right on, Brother! Tell it like it is! Amen!" But when the preacher condemned the sin of gossip, the two got quiet, and one turned to the other and said, "He's done quit preaching and now he's meddlin'."

A minister went to visit one of his congregants. He knocked on the door several times, but no one answered. He could see through the window that the television was on, so he took one of his cards, wrote "Revelation 3:20" on it, and stuck it in the door. (Revelation 3:20 says, "Behold, I stand at the door and knock; if anyone will open, I will come in.") The following Sunday a woman handed him a card with her name and the following message: "Genesis 3:10." (Genesis 3:10 says, "I heard thy voice and I was naked, so I hid myself.")

During the 1930s Thelma Goldstein from Chicago treated herself to her first real vacation in Florida. Being unfamiliar with the area, she wandered into a restricted hotel in North Miami. "Excuse me," she said to the manager, "My name is Mrs. Goldstein and I'd like a small room for two weeks." "I'm awfully sorry," he replied, "but all of our rooms are occupied." Just as he said that a man came down and checked out. "What luck," said Mrs. Goldstein. "Now there's a room." "Not so fast, madam. I'm sorry, but this hotel is restricted. No Jews allowed." "Jewish? Who's Jewish? I happen to be Catholic." "I find that hard to believe," said the manager. "Let me ask you, who was the Son of God?" "Jesus, Son of Mary." "Where was he born?" "In a stable." "And why was he born in a stable?" "Because a schmuck like you wouldn't let a Jew rent a room in his hotel?"

A Muslim, a Christian, and a Jew were having a discussion about who was the most religious. "I was riding my camel in the middle of the Sahara," exclaimed the Muslim. "Suddenly a fierce sandstorm appeared from nowhere. I truly thought my end had come as I lay next to my camel while we were buried deeper and deeper under the sand. But I did not lose my faith in the almighty Allah. I prayed and prayed and suddenly, for a hundred yards all around me, the storm had stopped. Since that day I am a devout Muslim and have learned to recite the Koran by memory."

"One day while fishing," said the Christian, "I was in my little dinghy in the middle of the ocean. Suddenly a fierce storm appeared from nowhere. I truly thought my end had come as my little dinghy was tossed up and down in the rough ocean. But I did not lose my faith in Jesus Christ. I prayed and prayed and suddenly, for three hundred yards all around me, the storm had stopped. Since that day I am a devout Christian teaching young children about Jesus." "One day I was walking down the road," explained the Jew. "I was in my most expensive designer outfit in the middle of New York City. Suddenly I saw a black bag appear out of nowhere. It was on the ground in front of me. I put my hand inside and found a million dollars in cash. I truly thought my end had come as it was a Saturday and we are not allowed to handle money on Saturdays. But I did not lose my faith in Jehovah. I prayed and prayed and suddenly, for five hundred yards all around me, it was Tuesday . . ."

A man was in his bed dying, slipping in and out of consciousness. His wife came into the room with his doctor and their parish priest. "Mrs. Kelleher, you realize that the bill for my services is one thousand dollars," the doctor said. "Fine," said the woman. "I'll see to it that it's paid from the insurance." "And don't forget, Mary, the funeral and casket will cost one thousand dollars," the priest said. "Don't worry, Father, I'll see to it that you're paid as well." The three walked over to the bed. The doctor stood on one side of the man and the priest stood on the other. The man opened his eyes and saw the two men there and said, "Father, would you tell the people at my funeral that I died as Jesus died?" "Do you mean pure of heart and poor in spirit, Tom?" "No, I mean between two thieves!"

Said the minister to the priest: "After all, we are both doing the Lord's work—you in your way, and I in His."

A woman was working really hard in her vegetable garden. It was quite a fabulous garden. It had been meticulously weeded, watered, and fertilized. The plants were all flourishing and beautiful. Her minister stopped by and remarked on what a beautiful garden it was, adding, "It's truly a miracle what the Lord can do in a garden." She paused and replied, "Well, maybe so, Pastor, but you should have seen the mess it was when He was taking care of it all by Himself."

$\mathcal{A}$ sweet young thing was telling the evangelist Jimmy Swaggert that she had been sleeping in another bedroom since she had caught her husband sleeping with the neighbor. "It's your duty to forgive him, my child," intoned Swaggert as he patted her hand, and she fell into his arms, gently sobbing. "But," he added as his grip tightened, "how'd you like to get even with the S.O.B. first?"

A rabbi who was late for a golf game was rather curt with several people whose phone calls kept delaying him. The next day his secretary said, "Rabbi, several members of the congregation were really upset with you when you cut them short yesterday." At that point, a man who had been sitting within earshot in the reception room got up and departed hurriedly. "Who was that?" asked the rabbi. "Oh, that was Mr. Rothenberg," she answered. "He wanted to speak to you about a circumcision for his son."

A priest had just finished hearing a man's confession and was considering the man's penitence. "Are you sure you're going to try to set aside all sin?" "Yes, Father, I certainly am going to try," replied the man. "I hereby resolve to double my efforts." "And you're going to attend mass regularly, my son?" the priest went on. "Yes, Father, I realize I have strayed," said the man. "I shall both worship and confess every week." "And how about your debts and those you have cheated?" inquired the priest. "Now just a minute, Father," said the man. "Now you're talking business, not religion."

A Hindu priest, a rabbi, and a lawyer were driving down a road when their car broke down. Fortunately, there was a farmhouse nearby, where the farmer informed them that he had only one spare room, and that it had only two twin beds. They were welcome to it, but one of them had to sleep in the barn. After much discussion, the Hindu volunteered to go to the barn. A few moments later there came a knock on the bedroom door, and the Hindu explained that there was a cow in the barn, and cows are sacred. He could not possibly sleep in the barn with a cow. Annoyed, the rabbi volunteered. A few minutes later there came another knock on the door. The rabbi explained that there was a pig in the barn and that he, being Orthodox, could not possibly spend the evening in a barn with the origin of pork. Finally, the lawyer said that he would go to the barn. A few minutes later there was yet another knock on the door. It was the cow and the pig!

A little outback village in Australia managed to buy a new fire engine. The village council, thinking they needed an official blessing but were unable to agree on how, invited a priest, a minister, and a rabbi. The moment of dedication came. The minister stood at the front of the engine and read a few psalms from the Bible. The priest stood on the driver's side and prayed a few prayers in Latin and sprinkled the new engine with holy water. The rabbi went around to the back of the fire engine, took a hacksaw from under his coat, and sawed six inches off the exhaust pipe.

A minister, a priest, and a rabbi went for a hike one day. It was very hot. They were sweating and exhausted when they came upon a small lake. Since it was fairly secluded, they took off all their clothes and jumped in the water. Feeling refreshed, the trio decided to pick a few berries while enjoying their freedom. As they were crossing an open area, who should come along but a group of ladies from town. Unable to get to their clothes in time, the minister and the priest covered their privates and the rabbi covered his face while they ran for cover. After the ladies had left and the men got their clothes back on, the minister and the priest asked the rabbi why he had covered his face rather than his privates. The rabbi replied, "I don't know about you, but in my congregation, it's my face they would recognize."

A minister, a priest, and a rabbi were playing poker when the police raided the game. Turning to the minister, the lead police officer said, "Reverend Allsworth, were you gambling?" Turning his eyes to heaven, the minister whispered, "Lord, forgive me for what I am about to do." To the police officer he then said, "No, officer, I was not gambling." The officer then asked the priest, "Father Murphy, were you gambling?" Again, after an appeal to heaven, the priest replied, "No, officer, I was not gambling." Turning to the rabbi, the officer again asked, "Rabbi Goldstein, were you gambling?" Shrugging his shoulders, the rabbi replied, "With whom?"

$\mathcal{A}$ minister, a priest, and a rabbi are sitting around a dinner table having a heated argument about religion. Suddenly, an angel of the Lord appears and says, "I will grant one wish to each of you!" The minister jumps to his feet and shouts, "I wish for the destruction of all Catholics!" Then the priest jumps to his feet and shouts, "Well, I wish for the destruction of all Protestants!" The angel turns to the rabbi and says, "What do you wish for, rabbi?" And the rabbi says, "Well, if you're going to grant their wishes, then I'll just have another cup of coffee!"

$\mathcal{A}$ minister, a rabbi, and a priest were at some sort of ecumenical gathering. As they were seated at the same conference table, their discussion got around to problems in their respective houses of worship. All three of them had problems with bats in the belfry. The minister admitted that he had actually crawled up there and shot them. But then he had holes in the roof and had to have that repaired. The rabbi said that he had set traps for the bats but they still came back. The priest said that he baptized the bats, then confirmed them, and he hadn't seen them since.

A middle-aged woman has a heart attack and is taken to the hospital. While on the operating table she has a near-death experience. During that experience she sees God and asks if this is it. God says no and explains that she has another thirty years to live. Upon her recovery she decides to just stay in the hospital and have a facelift, liposuction, breast augmentation, tummy tuck, and so on. She even has someone come in and change her hair color. She figures since she's got another thirty years, she might as well make the most of it. She walks out of the hospital after the last operation and is killed by an ambulance speeding up to the hospital. She arrives in front of God and complains: "I thought you said I had another thirty years!" God replies, "I didn't recognize you."

An atheist is sitting on a park bench when a priest walks over and sits down. The atheist says to the priest, "How can you believe in God? You know nothing like that can exist!" The priest says, "How can you say something like that, my son? Of course God exists! Look at his work all around you!" The atheist replies, "You know what I mean. The world is so incongruous, there's no way it was created by God. Take the hummingbird. It spends its life flitting from flower to flower, but it doesn't need to go very far from where it was born to find food. It can live its entire life in a small area, yet it can fly around the world! And then look at the hippo. Big, ungainly, needs hundreds of pounds of food every day, but can't get very far to go find it. Yet that hippo, who needs to be able to move much more freely, can't fly! 'Why can't hippos fly?" Just then a bird flies by and drops an unsavory load right between the atheist's eyes. The priest says, "I guess you just got your answer."

$\mathscr{A}$ lady bought a parrot from a pet store, only to find after taking the bird home that the bird would say nothing but "My name is Mary and I'm a whore." Weeks of trying to teach the bird other phrases proved useless. The bird still dropped the same line, usually at the most inopportune moments, much to the lady's embarrassment. One day her parish priest dropped by for a visit and, sure enough, while he was there the parrot squawked out the only words it would say. After apologizing profusely to the priest, the lady explained her bird resisted all efforts at reformation. The priest offered to take the bird to visit the two birds he had, as all his birds would say were Hail Marys while clutching rosaries in their talons. He was certain they would have a good influence on the lady's bird. So he took the parrot to his house and put it in the cage with his two birds, and the first words out of the newcomer's mouth were, "My name is Mary and I'm a whore." The priest, being most anxious to see what would happen, was dumbfounded when one of his birds said to the other, "Throw that damned rosary away! Our prayers have been answered!"

$\mathcal{M}$iss Bingham was in her eighties and much admired for her sweetness and kindness to all. Her minister came to call one afternoon early in the spring and she welcomed him into her Victorian parlor. She invited him to have a seat while she prepared a little tea. As he sat facing her old pump organ, the minister noticed a cut-glass bowl sitting on top of it filled with water. In the water floated, of all things, a condom. Imagine his shock and surprise. Imagine his curiosity! Surely Miss Bingham had flipped—or something. But he certainly couldn't mention the strange sight in her parlor. When she returned with tea and cookies, they began to chat. The minister tried to stifle his curiosity about the bowl of water and its strange floater, but soon it got the better of him and he could resist no longer. "Miss

Bingham," he said, "I wonder if you would tell me about this." He pointed to the bowl. "Oh, yes," she replied, "isn't it wonderful? I was walking downtown last fall and I found this little package. It said to put it on your organ and keep it wet and it would prevent disease. And you know, I think it's working. I haven't had a cold all winter."

A friend asks God where he's going on holiday this year and God replies, "Certainly not earth again. I went there about two millennia ago and got some girl pregnant, and they haven't stopped talking about it since!"

How can you make God laugh?
Tell Him your plans for the future.

Three nuns who had recently died were on their way to heaven. At the pearly gates they were met by St. Peter. Around the gates there was a collection of lights and bells. St. Peter stopped them and told them that they would each have to answer a question before they could enter the pearly gates. St. Peter asked, "What were the names of the two people in the Garden of Eden?" The first nun said, "Adam and Eve." The lights flashed, the bells rang, and in she went through the pearly gates. Then St. Peter asked the second nun, "What did Adam eat from the forbidden tree?" The nun replied, "An apple." The lights flashed, the bells rang, and in she went through the pearly gates. And finally it was the third nun's turn. St. Peter asked, "What was the first thing Eve said to Adam?" After a few minutes thinking, she shook her head from side to side and said, "Gosh, that's a hard one!" The lights flashed, the bells rang, and in she went through the pearly gates.

Heaven is where:

The police are British

The mechanics are German

The cooks are French

The lovers are Italian

And the whole thing is organized by the Swiss.

Hell is where:

The police are German

The cooks are British

The mechanics are French

The lovers are Swiss

And the whole thing is organized by the Italians.

A minister dies and is waiting in line at the pearly gates. Ahead of him is a guy who's dressed in sunglasses, a loud shirt, leather jacket, and jeans. St. Peter addresses this guy: "Who are you so that I may know whether or not to admit you to the kingdom of heaven?" The guy replies, "I'm Joe Hoffman, taxi driver in Noo Yawk City." St. Peter consults his list. He smiles and says to the taxi driver, "Take this silken robe and golden staff and enter the kingdom of heaven." The taxi driver goes into heaven with his robe and staff, and now it's the minister's turn. He stands erect and booms out, "I am

186

Joseph Snow, pastor of St. Mary's for the last forty-three years." St. Peter consults his list. He says to the minister, "Take this cotton robe and wooden staff and enter the kingdom of heaven." "Just a minute," says the minister. "That man was a taxi driver and he got a silken robe and golden staff. How can this be?" "Up here we work by results," says St. Peter. "While you preached, people slept. While he drove, people prayed."

$\mathcal{A}$ wealthy man died and proceeded to go to heaven. At the pearly gates he was met by St. Peter, who asked him whether he wanted to go to heaven or hell. He gave him a chance to take a tour of both and decide for himself. First, he was taken to heaven, where he was shown people praying and, in general, leading a very austere kind of existence. Then he was taken on a grand tour of hell, where he saw people were drinking and having a good time. There were lots of good-looking women and, in general, a lot of merrymaking. When taken back to St. Peter, he asked to be put in hell. Suddenly, a huge servant from hell pulled him gruffly by the arm and took him down below. But he was shocked to see that everywhere people were being tortured, and he saw boiling oil and devilish creatures. He exclaimed to the attendant, "This was not what I was shown a short while ago!" To this the attendant laughed and replied, "Oh, that was just the infomercial."

The British Intelligence Chief (M.) sends James Bond on a secret mission to heaven. When M. doesn't hear from Bond for over a day, he gets worried and calls up heaven. Virgin Mary picks up the phone and says, "Virgin Mary speaking." M. asks her if Bond has reached there yet, and she says no. M. waits another few hours and calls heaven back again. "Virgin Mary speaking," comes the response. "Is James there yet?" asks M., and the response is no again. M. is really worried by this time, but he waits for a few more hours and then calls heaven back again. He is relieved to hear, "Mary here."

Chaucer and Shakespeare died. St. Peter told them there was only one spot remaining in heaven. The one to compose the best four-liner ending in "Timbuktu" could get into heaven. They came back a day later and Shakespeare recited:

> Two caravans in the desert heat,
> Their paths crossed and they did meet,
> Side by side, two by two,
> They headed off to Timbuktu.

Chaucer grinned and recited:

> We were in the desert,
>   my friend Tim and I,
> A maidens' harem we did spy,
> But they were three and we were two,
> So I bucked one and Tim bucked two!

Guess who got into heaven.

A Catholic, a Jew, and an Episcopalian are lined up at the entrance to heaven. The Catholic asks to get in and God says, "Nope, sorry." "Why not?" asks the Catholic. "I've been good." "Well, you ate meat on a Friday in Lent, so I can't let you in." The Jew walks up and God refuses him too. The Jew wants an explanation so God replies, "There was that time you ate pork. Sorry, but I can't let you in either." Then the Episcopalian goes up and asks to be let in, and God again says no. "Why not?" asks the Episcopalian. "What did I do wrong?" "Well," says God, "you once ate your entrée with the salad fork."

A rabbi, a priest, and a minister were on their way to Pittsburgh for an ecumenical convention. When they arrived at the airport, all three were taken aback by the scantily clad, buxom woman behind the counter. After a brief moment of hesitation, the rabbi very nervously approached the counter and said, "I want three pickets to Tittsburg." To help cover the embarrassment of his comrade, the minister stepped in to save the day. He handled himself pretty well, until he said he wanted his 35 cents' change as a quarter and two nipples. As they were leaving, the priest decided that he should do the Christian thing and advise the young woman that her apparel was inappropriate. He said, "Young lady, you really need to do something about your appearance. If you don't, when you get to the gates of heaven, St. Finger will shake his peter at you!"

This guy dies and gets sent down to hell. When he arrives, Satan meets him in the reception room and says to him, "Okay, now you've got to choose the room in which you will spend the rest of eternity." He points to three doors on the other side of the room. The guy goes through the first door. Beyond is a vast room with a concrete floor. The room is full of people standing on their heads. "That floor looks a bit hard," says the guy. "I think I'll try the next door." So he tries the next door and finds himself in another vast room, this time with a wooden floor. Again, the room is full of people standing on their heads. "I don't like the look of this," he says. "I'd get splinters of wood in my head."

So he tries the third and final door. This time, the room is full of people sitting on chairs knee-deep in shit, eating biscuits and drinking cups of tea. "Hmm," he says to himself. "I suppose that spending eternity sitting on a chair with my legs dangling in shit isn't such a bad thing. At least I'll have something to eat and drink." So he goes back to where Satan is waiting for him and tells him the decision he has made. "Very well," says Satan, "you shall spend eternity in the third room." And he escorts the guy back to the door. As he opens the door he hears a voice shouting, "Okay everybody, tea break's over. Back on your heads!"

$\mathcal{A}$ small manufacturing company in the Northwest, Anderson Nails, had been experiencing years of success and growth. Feeling the company was ready to try for the big time, the owner, Mr. Anderson, contracted a big Madison Avenue advertising agency to help him promote his product. Aiming to get the greatest possible exposure, the agency booked a full minute at the beginning of the Super Bowl's halftime show. Anderson was pretty excited about this, and invited all of his friends and relatives to his home for a big Super Bowl party. At the end of the first half, everybody drew closer to the TV, waiting to see the premiere of the commercial. It began with an aerial shot of the desert and zoomed in on a small walled city. As the camera slowly panned about the city, it became apparent that this was Jerusalem during the Roman occupation. A large hill on the horizon came into view and as the camera drew closer, a number of crosses became visible. The focus settled on a naked man in a crown of thorns, then moved in for an extreme closeup of his bleeding hands and the nails that held them to the cross. Clearly visible were the words Manufactured by Anderson Nails. A subtitle appeared on the screen bearing the words, "Anderson Nails—The Expert's Choice." Anderson's guests were horrified. The party broke up before the end of the game. The next day he began to get phone calls from his oldest and most loyal customers, expressing their outrage and canceling their orders. By the end of the week, his sales were down to nothing. He called the president of the advertising agency to cancel his contract. When Anderson explained the situation, the ad man was surprised and offered to run a new campaign at no charge. The new campaign was slated to start in a few weeks' time. This time, Anderson nervously watched the commercial alone in the privacy of his office. It began the same way as before, with an aerial view of Jerusalem. The camera finally settled on two Roman soldiers drinking wine at a table near the marketplace. Hearing a disturbance nearby, they looked up from their drinks in time to see a naked man with bleeding hands and feet being pursued by a group of soldiers. The first soldier looked at his companion, smiled knowingly, and said, "I bet they didn't use Anderson Nails!"

man in middle age became fed up with humanity and decided to spend the rest of his life in a monastery. The abbot warned him that he would have to take a vow of silence and live the rest of his life as a scribe, to which the man replied, "No problem. I'm sick of talking." Ten years went by and the abbot called for the man. He told him that he was a model monk and perfect scribe, and that they were very happy to have him. As per their tradition, he was allowed to say two words. Asked if he had anything to say, the man nodded and said, "Food cold." The abbot sent him on his way. Ten years later he was brought before the abbot again and once again was told how pleased they were with his performance. He was again allowed two more words if he so chose. The man said, "Bed hard," and was sent back to work. Another ten years went by and again the abbot sent for the man, telling him that he was the best monk they had ever had, and that he was allowed another two words. The man nodded and said, "I quit." To this the abbot replied in a disgusted tone, "Doesn't surprise me. You've done nothing but complain since you got here."

A priest was feeling despondent over being posted to a dry, desert parish. He wrote letters to his bishop constantly requesting that he be posted somewhere more hospitable. No reply ever came, and soon he stopped sending his letters. Years later, when the archbishop was making the rounds of the rural churches, he stopped in to see how the unhappy priest was doing. He found a pleasant man in an air-conditioned church. There were no parishioners, since the closest neighbors were many miles away. The archbishop admitted to some confusion, since the priest did not look like the desperate writer of so many unhappy letters. He asked the priest how he liked it out in the desert. "At first I was unhappy. But thanks to two things I have grown to love it here in the sparse desert." "And they are?" the archbishop inquired. "The first is my rosary. Without my rosary I wouldn't make it a day out here." "And the second?" At this the priest looked nervous. "Well, to be honest, I have developed a taste for martinis in the afternoon. They help to alleviate the heat during the worst part of the day." He looked sheepish at this admission, but the archbishop just smiled. "Martinis, eh? Well, that's not so bad. In fact, I'd be glad to share one with you right now, if you don't mind, that is." "Not at all!" The priest smiled. "Let me get one for you right away." Turning to the back of the church, the priest shouted "Oh, Rosary . . ."

On one sunny Sunday in spring, Father Fitzpatrick noticed that there was a smaller gathering than usual for the noon service. So as soon as the final hymn was sung, he slipped out the back way and went along the street to see who was out and about instead of coming to church. The first person he saw was old Mrs. O'Neil sitting on a park bench with her cane beside her. The good cleric sat down next to her and said, "Good afternoon, Mrs. O'Neil. Why weren't you in church today?" Mrs. O'Neil replied, "Well, Father, it was just such a lovely day today I didn't want to be cooped up in that stuffy ol' church!" The priest was a bit taken aback by this blunt answer, so he thought for a minute then asked, "But Mrs. O'Neil, don't you want to go to heaven?" To his surprise the elderly lady shook her head vehemently and said, "No siree!"

At that the priest got to his feet indignantly and said firmly, "You don't want to go to heaven? Then I am ashamed of you!" Now it was Mrs. O'Neil's turn to be surprised. She looked up at him and said, "Oh, Father, I thought you were leaving right now!"

The pope was scheduled to visit Memphis, and when his plane landed at the airport he stepped onto the tarmac to hear cries of "Elvis! Elvis!" The pope looked around to see who they were shouting at and said, "I'm the pope, not Elvis." Off he went in his limo. Throughout the city he heard people shout, "Elvis! Elvis!" He said, "I'm the pope, not Elvis! Can't you see, I'm wearing the hat, the robe, and the cross. I'm the pope!" He eventually got to his hotel and as he walked into the lobby, the hotel manager said, "Whoa, King." The pope said for the last time, "I'm the pope, not Elvis!" Looking very annoyed, the pope went up to his hotel room. As he entered, sitting on his bed was a gorgeous redhead looking very seductive. She sighed to him, "Oh, Elvis!" The pope got down on one knee and sang, "Wella blessa my soul, whatsa wrong with me."

One day Sister Marie was fishing and caught a huge fish for supper. A man was walking by and said, "Wow, what a goddamn fish!" The sister said, "Sir, you shouldn't talk to me like that. I'm a nun." The man said, "But that's the name of it, a goddamn fish." So the sister took the fish back to the rectory and said, "Mother Superior, look at the goddamn fish I caught." The mother superior said, "Sister, you shouldn't talk like that!" The sister said, "But Mother Superior, that's the name of it, a goddamn fish." So the mother superior said, "Well, give me the goddamn fish and I'll clean it." While she was cleaning the fish, the monsignor walked in and she said, "Monsignor, look at the goddamn fish that Sister Marie caught." The monsignor said, "Mother Superior, you shouldn't talk like that!" The mother superior said, "But that's the name of it, a goddamn fish." So the monsignor said, "Well, give me the goddamn fish and I'll cook it." That evening at supper there was a new priest at the table and he said, "Wow, what a nice fish." Sister Marie said, "I caught the goddamn fish." The mother superior said, "I cleaned the goddamn fish." The monsignor said, "I cooked the goddamn fish." And the new priest said, "I like this fucking place already!"

A nun and a priest were traveling across the desert when the camel they were using for transportation died. They set up a makeshift camp, hoping someone would come to their rescue, but to no avail. They prayed a lot and they discussed their predicament in great depth. Finally, the priest said to the nun, "You know, Sister, I am about to die and there's always been one thing I wanted here on earth—to see a woman naked. Would you mind taking off your clothes so I can look at you?" The nun thought about this request for several seconds and then agreed to take off her clothes. As she was doing so, she remarked, "Well, Father, now that I think about it,

"I've never seen a man naked either. Would you mind taking off your clothes too?" With little hesitation the priest also stripped. Suddenly the nun exclaimed, "Father! What is that little thing hanging between your legs?" The priest patiently answered, "That, my child, is a gift from God. If I put it in you, it creates a new life." "Well, for God's sake," responded the nun, "forget about me. Stick it in the camel!"

Sister Catherine is asking all the Catholic schoolchildren in the fourth grade what they want to be when they grow up. Little Sheila says, "When I grow up I want to be a prostitute." Sister Catherine's eyes grow wide and she barks, "What did you say?" "A prostitute," Sheila repeats. Sister Catherine breathes a sigh of relief and says, "Thank God! I thought you said a Protestant."

Three nuns are walking down the street when a man jumps out and flashes them. The first nun has a stroke, the second nun has a stroke, the third one didn't touch him.

A nun is driving the convent's car through some very lonely countryside when the car runs out of gas. She walks to the nearest filling station but forgets to take along the canister for the gas. The nice guy at the filling station has no canister either. He thinks for a while then hands her a chamber pot full of gas. The nun walks back to her car and starts pouring the gas from the chamber pot into the tank. A bypassing car stops, and the driver looks out and says wistfully, "Sister, how I would like to have as much faith as you do!"

$\mathcal{A}$ nun was walking in the convent when one of the priests noticed she was gaining a little weight. "Gaining a little weight, are we, Sister Margaret?" he asked. "Oh, no, Father. Just a little gas," Sister Margaret explained matter-of-factly. A month or so later the priest noticed that she had gained even more weight. "Gaining some weight, are we, Sister Margaret?" he asked again. "Oh no, Father. Just a little gas," she replied again. A couple of months later the priest noticed Sister Margaret pushing a baby carriage around the convent. He leaned over and looked in the carriage and said, "Cute little fart."

A very religious man lived right next door to an atheist. While the religious man prayed day in and day out and was constantly on his knees in communion with the Lord, the atheist never even looked twice at a church. However, the atheist's life was good; he had a well-paying job and a beautiful wife, and his children were healthy and good-natured, whereas the pious man's job was strenuous and his wages were low, his wife was getting fatter every day, and his kids wouldn't give him the time of day. So one day, deep in prayer as usual, he raised his eyes toward heaven and asked, "Oh God, I honor You every day, I ask Your advice for every problem, and confess to You my every sin. Yet my neighbor, who doesn't even believe in You and certainly never prays, seems blessed with every happiness while I go poor and suffer every indignity. Why is this?" And a great voice was heard from above: "*Because he doesn't bother me!*"

$\mathcal{A}$ Jew is dying and he asks, "Are you there, dear wife?" She answers, "Why yes, my love." Then he asks, "Are you there, beloved son?" His son says, "Yes, I am, Father." So the father asks, "Then who the hell is minding the store?"

An old Albanian is dying. His entire family is gathered around him. When he comes to, he asks everybody but his eldest son to leave. When they are alone, he says, "Look after the Jews." The son, taken aback, says, "Father, don't you have anything more important to say to me at this moment?" The Father repeats, "Look after the Jews. When they're finished with them, it will be our turn."

One day a minister goes to a barber for a haircut. After the haircut, he asks the barber how much he owes. The barber says, "For a man of the cloth, the haircut is free!" The minister thinks, "What a nice man!" The next day the barber finds a case of wine outside his shop. Then a priest comes in for a haircut. Again, the barber tells him that the haircut is free. The priest thinks, "What a nice man!" The next day the barber finds a box of chocolates outside his shop. Then a rabbi comes in for a haircut. Again, the barber gives the haircut on the house. The rabbi thinks, "What a nice man!" The next day, the barber finds a long line of rabbis outside his shop!

An elderly southern widow who lived in a large mansion felt generous when it came to Thanksgiving. She called up the local military base and asked to speak to the lieutenant. "Please send up four nice young men to eat dinner here on Thanksgiving. But please, don't send any Jews. Please, no Jews." The lieutenant replied, "No problem, ma'am, and I am sure I speak for the army when I say we all appreciate your kindness." Well, Thanksgiving rolled around, and the widow went to answer the door when it rang. She was surprised to see four of the blackest boys that anyone had ever seen, especially in the South. "But, but, there must be some mistake," she stammered. One of them replied, "No, ma'am. Lieutenant Goldstein doesn't make mistakes."

Two Jewish guys, Marcus and Irving, are walking down the street when Irving decides that he needs a new suit. So they stop in at Pinkus the tailor to have a suit made. Pinkus takes a sample suit from the back and says, "This is the latest fashion and it's a bargain!" Irving asks if it is available in black. Pinkus says, "Of course," so he agrees to buy it. As he leaves, he reminds Pinkus to make the suit in black. The next week the two guys go back to Pinkus to pick up the suit. Irving looks at it very closely and says, "I think this is dark blue, not black! What do you think, Marcus?" "It looks blue to me," says Marcus. Pinkus assures them that it is indeed black. So Irving pays, puts on the suit, and they leave the store. However, he remains unconvinced. As they walk down the street, Irving says, "I have an idea about how we can check the suit. There are two nuns coming toward us in their black habits. Let's kind of push up against them so we can check to see if the suit is really black." So as Marcus and Irving pass the nuns, they push up against them. The guys apologize to the nuns and take off. The first nun turns to the other and says, "I wonder what that was all about?" The second nun says, "They looked Jewish, but I wasn't sure." "Why not?" "Because one of them spoke Latin." "Latin? How? What did he say?" "I didn't catch all of it, but what I heard sounded like, 'Marcus Pinkus Fuckedus'!"

The Vatican ambassador in Paris was complaining to a French official, "You know, it's rough being a diplomat. I get invited to these parties where everyone stands around with a small plate of canapés trying not to look bored. Then in walks a shapely woman in a low-cut, revealing gown, and everyone in the whole place turns around and looks—at me!"

A minister, a priest, and a rabbi were discussing when life begins. The priest said that life began at conception, while the minister believed that life began at birth. Then the rabbi, after pondering this question for a while, looked up and said, "Life begins when the kids move out and the dog is dead!"

After a major religious revival had concluded, the three pastors were discussing the results with one another. The Methodist minister said, "The revival worked out great for us! We gained four new families." The Baptist preacher said, "We did better than that! We gained six new families." The Presbyterian pastor said, "Well, we did even better than that! We got rid of our ten biggest troublemakers!"

$\mathcal{A}$ mother was preparing pancakes for her two young sons. The boys began to argue over who would get the first pancake. Their mother saw the opportunity for a moral lesson. "If Jesus were sitting here He would say, 'Let my brother have the first pancake, I can wait.'" The older brother turned to his younger brother and said, "Okay, you be Jesus!"

A minister told his congregation, "Next week I plan to preach about the sin of lying. To help you understand my sermon, I want you all to read Mark 17." The following Sunday, as he prepared to deliver his sermon, the minister asked for a show of hands. He wanted to know how many had read Mark 17. Every hand went up. The minister smiled and said, "Mark has only sixteen chapters. I will now proceed to preach on the sin of lying."

Yeshiva University decided to field a crew team. Unfortunately, they lost race after race. They practiced for hours every day but never managed to come in any better than dead last. The university finally decided to send Yankel to spy on the Harvard team. So Yankel schlepped off to Cambridge and hid in the bushes off the Charles River, where he carefully watched the Harvard team as they practiced. Yankel finally returned to Yeshiva University. "I have figured out their secret," he announced. "They have eight guys *rowing* and only one guy *shouting*."

Meyer, a lonely widower, was walking home one day, wishing something wonderful would happen in his life, when he passed a pet store and heard a squawking voice shouting out in Yiddish: "Quawwwk . . . vus macht du . . . yeah, you . . . outside, standing like a schmuck . . . eh?" Meyer rubbed his eyes and ears. He couldn't believe it! The proprietor flung open the door and grabbed Meyer by the sleeve. "Come in here, fella, and check out this parrot." Meyer stood in front of the African Grey that cocked his little head and said, "Vus? Kenst reddin Yiddish?" Meyer turned excitedly to the store owner. "He speaks Yiddish?" "What did you expect? Chinese, maybe?" In a matter of moments, Meyer had put five hundred dollars down on the counter and carried the parrot in his cage away with him. All night he talked with the parrot in Yiddish. He told the parrot about his father's adventures coming to America, about how beautiful his mother was when she was a young bride, about his family, about his years of working in the garment center, and about Florida. The parrot listened and commented. They shared some walnuts. The parrot told him of living in the pet store, how he hated the weekends. Then they both went to sleep. Next morning, Meyer began saying his prayers. The parrot demanded to know what he was doing, and when Meyer explained, the parrot wanted to pray too. Meyer went out and made a miniature yarmulke for the parrot. The parrot wanted to learn to read Hebrew so Meyer spent weeks and months sitting and teaching the parrot the Torah. In time, Meyer came to love and count on the parrot as a friend and a Jew. He was lonely no more. One morning on Rosh Hashanah, Meyer rose and got dressed and was about to leave when the parrot demanded to go with him. Meyer explained that a synagogue was not a place for a bird, but the parrot made a terrific argument and was carried to the synagogue on Meyer's shoulder. Needless to say, they made quite a spectacle, and Meyer was questioned by everyone, including the rabbi. At first, he refused to allow a bird into the building on the High Holy Days, but Meyer convinced him to let him in this one time, swearing that the parrot could pray. Wagers were made with Meyer. Thousands of dollars were bet that the parrot could *not* pray, could not speak Yiddish or Hebrew, and so on. All eyes were on the African Grey during services. The parrot perched on Meyer's shoulder as one prayer and song passed—Meyer heard not a peep from the bird. He began to become annoyed, slapping at his shoulder and mumbling under his breath, "Pray already!" The parrot said nothing. "Pray . . . Parrot, you can pray, so pray . . . come on, everybody's looking at you!" The parrot said nothing. After Rosh Hashanah services were concluded, Meyer found that he owed his synagogue buddies and the rabbi over four thousand dollars. He marched home, pissed off, saying nothing. Finally, several blocks from the temple, the bird began to sing an old Yiddish song and was happy as a lark. Meyer stopped and looked at him. "You miserable bird, you cost me over four thousand dollars. Why? After I taught you the morning prayers, and taught you to read Hebrew and the Torah. And after you begged me to bring you to a synagogue on Rosh Hashanah. Why? Why did you do this to me?" "Don't be a schmuck," the parrot replied. "Think of the odds on Yom Kippur!"

$\mathcal{A}$ small girl was reprimanded by her mother for laughing while saying her bedtime prayers. "It's okay, Mom," she explained. "I was just sharing a joke with God."

A new family begins visiting the First Baptist Church in town. Someone on the board of deacons for the Ladies' Home Auxiliary notices that they dress a bit "scruffy." All agree that it would be best to help out by providing the new family with some church-going clothes, and a collection is taken up. The new clothes are bought and donated to the family, upon which time they stop attending church. Finally, the pastor pays a visit. "We don't see you in church anymore, Brother Smith. Anything wrong?" queries the pastor. "Not a bit," responds the newcomer. "Since we look so nice in these new clothes, we've been attending St. Michael's Episcopal Church."

$\mathcal{A}$ctual announcements taken from Presbyterian church bulletins:

1. Don't let worry kill you—let the church help.

2. Thursday night—potluck supper. Prayer and medication to follow.

3. Remember in prayer the many who are sick of our church and community.

4. For those of you who have children and don't know it, we have a nursery downstairs.

5. The rosebud on the altar this morning is to announce the birth of David Alan Belter, the sin of Rev. and Mrs. Julius Belter.

6. This afternoon there will be a meeting in the south and north ends of the church. Children will be baptized at both ends.

7. Tuesday at 4:00 P.M. there will be an ice cream social. All ladies giving milk will please come early.

8. Wednesday the Ladies' Liturgy Society will meet. Mrs. Jones will sing, "Put Me in My Little Bed" accompanied by the pastor.

9. Thursday at 5:00 P.M. there will be a meeting of the Little Mothers' Club. All wishing to become little mothers, please see the minister in his study.

10. This being Easter Sunday, we will ask Mrs. Miller to come forward and lay an egg on the altar.

11. Next Sunday a special collection will be taken to defray the cost of the new carpet. All those wishing to do something on the new carpet will come forward and do so.

12. The ladies of the church have cast off clothing of every kind and they may be seen in the church basement Friday.

13. A bean supper will be held on Tuesday evening in the church hall. Music will follow.

14. At the evening service tonight, the sermon topic will be "What Is Hell?" Come early and listen to our choir practice.

Taoism: Shit happens.

Protestantism: Let shit happen to
someone else.

Catholicism: If shit happens, you
deserve it.

Judaism: Why does shit always
happen to us?

Atheism: No shit.

TV Evangelism: Send more shit.

Buddhism: What is the sound of
shit happening?

Hinduism: This shit happened
before.

There was a sizable graffito on the wall of Grand Central Station in New York: JESUS LIVES! Below it, in smaller lettering, someone had put the question, DOES THIS MEAN WE DON'T GET AN EASTER HOLIDAY?

Did you hear about the dyslexic rabbi? He walks around saying, "Yo."

A Sunday school teacher was discussing the Ten Commandments with her five- and six-year-olds. After explaining the commandment to "honor thy father and thy mother," she asked, "Is there a commandment that teaches us how to treat our brothers and sisters?" Without missing a beat, one boy, the oldest of a family of seven, answered, "Thou shalt not kill."

priest was preparing a man for his long day's journey into night. Whispering firmly, the priest said, "Denounce the devil! Let him know how little you think of his evil!" The dying man said nothing. The priest repeated his order. Still the dying man said nothing. The priest asked, "Why do you refuse to denounce the devil and his evil?" The dying man said, "Until I know where I'm heading, I don't think I should mix in."

What do you get when you cross a Jehovah's Witness with an atheist? Somebody who knocks on your door for no apparent reason.

Two businessmen seated on an airplane noticed a Catholic nun sitting in front of them. One of the men said to the other with a wink, "I was going to go to Ireland until I found out that half the country is Catholic, so I don't want to go there." The other man said, "Well, how about Poland, then?" The other man said, "No way. Poland is loaded with those Catholics too." The other man suggested a trip to the United States, but his companion said, "The Catholics have spread out over the whole country. Every time I turn around there, I bump into one." The men were watching and could see that the nun was fidgeting and getting kind of agitated about their conversation. The fellow who started the teasing decided to really get her mad and said, "I really wanted to go to Italy, but that place is crawling with Catholics, what with the pope there and all." At this the nun had had it and finally turned around in her seat and sweetly said to the men, "Why don't you both go to hell? I hear that there aren't any Catholics there!"

Two beggars are sitting on a park bench in Mexico City. One is holding a cross and one a Star of David. Both are holding hats to collect contributions. People walk by, lift their noses at the man with the Star of David, and drop money in the hat held by the man with the cross. Soon the hat of the man with the cross is filled, and the hat of the man with the Star of David is still empty. A priest watches and then approaches the men. He turns to the man with the Star of David and says, "Young man, don't you realize that this is a Catholic country? You'll never get any contributions in this country holding a Star of David." The man with the Star of David turns to the man with the cross and says, "Moishe, can you imagine, this guy is trying to tell us how to run our business?"

$\mathcal{A}$t a mass at which some young ladies were to take their final vows to become nuns, the bishop presiding noticed two rabbis enter the church just before the service began. They insisted on sitting on the right side of the center aisle. The bishop wondered why they had come, but he didn't have time to inquire before the mass began. When it came time for the announcements, the bishop's curiosity got the better of him. He welcomed the two rabbis and asked why they had chosen to be present at this occasion where the young ladies were to become the brides of Christ. The elder of the rabbis slowly rose to his feet and explained, "Family of the groom."

A journalist assigned to the Jerusalem bureau takes an apartment overlooking the Wailing Wall. Every day when she looks out, she sees an old Jewish man praying vigorously. So the journalist goes down and introduces herself to the old man. She asks, "You come every day to the wall. How long have you done that and what are you praying for?" The old man replies, "I have come here to pray every day for twenty-five years. In the morning I pray for world peace and then for the brotherhood of man. I go home, have a glass of tea, and I come back and pray for the eradication of illness and disease from the earth." The journalist is amazed. "How does it make you feel to come here every day for twenty-five years and pray for these things?" she asks. The old man looks at her sadly. "Like I'm talking to a wall."

Thank God I'm an atheist!